楠帯刀正行
市川團十郎

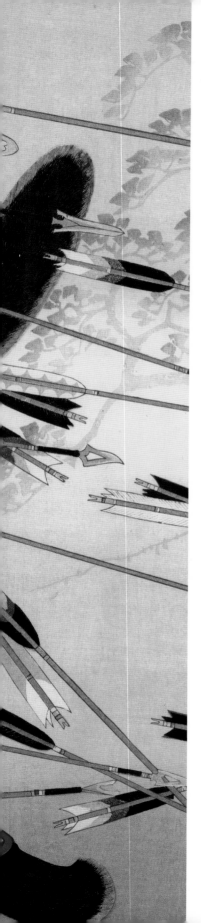

AN ILLUSTRATED GUIDE TO
SAMURAI
HISTORY AND CULTURE

From the Age of Musashi to Contemporary Pop Culture

Gavin Blair

Foreword by
Alexander Bennett

TUTTLE Publishing

Tokyo | Rutland, Vermont | Singapore

CONTENTS

LEFT A mounted samurai in full cavalry *o-yoroi* armor by a castle wall depicted in an Edo period print *Sixty-Nine Post Stations of the Kisokaido*. This is the ninth station, Kumagaya and the samurai Kojiro Naoie is pictured.

歌川 国芳 Utagawa Kuniyoshi (1798–1861)

THE SAMURAI MYSTIQUE

There is no higher praise in Japan today than to be called a samurai. The designation is usually reserved for people who have overcome great odds, and who demonstrate magnanimity and composure amid adversity. Although samurai status was abolished a century-and-a-half ago, nothing represents the masculine ideal more aptly to modern Japanese. Even national sports teams carry on their name: Samurai Blue (soccer) and Samurai Japan (baseball). There is nothing particularly thrilling about being called a farmer, even though it was they who made up the backbone of Japanese society throughout history by keeping the rest of it alive!

The attraction to samurai is certainly not limited to Japanese people. Since Japan opened its doors to the world following the Meiji Restoration of 1868, Westerners have been fascinated by the imagery and culture of Japan's feudal warrior, which combines extreme violence with selflessness and profound beauty. Incomprehensible customs such as seppuku, or ritual suicide by cutting one's abdomen open, appalled observers. At the same time, the fortitude of mind, the poetry, literature, and art shaped by these men-of-war have been lauded as being nothing short of phenomenal. The sensitivity exhibited was genuine, and emanated from embracing the evanescence of one's existence.

There were many paradoxes in the world of the samurai. I am reminded of a popular teaching in budo (Japanese martial arts, which are the most obvious vestige of samurai culture in the world today): *Do-chu-sei*—Calmness within movement. This is the state in which the body is moving energetically, but the mind remains perfectly calm. The opposite is called *sei-chu-do*—movement within calmness—in which the mind is primed for attack, but the body is completely still. From a historical perspective, this notion equates to chaos in order, and order in chaos.

ABOVE **Suzuki Magoichi (aka Saiga Magoichi) led one of the Ikko-Ikki bands of peasants and their allies who fought the samurai in the 16th century.**

月岡 芳年 **Tsukioka Yoshitoshi (1839-1892)**

The samurai embodied an unquenchable desire to enhance the name of their family and were fiercely competitive in ensuring that their pristine reputations would last for posterity. In this sense, their interminable quest for honor became inextricably linked to combat prowess and demonstrations of unremitting valor. For this reason, their seven centuries as the political rulers of Japan are characterized by the balancing of chaos and order. For example, the principle of *bunbu-ryodo*—the brush and sword in accord—i.e., proficiency in both the ways of literary and military arts, became a mainstay of the samurai ideal. In other words, the warrior's sensibilities, which were refined through appreciation and knowledge of the finer things in life, served as a counterbalance to the cruel realties of the violent world he inhabited.

To help him subjugate the chaos in his mind, the samurai lived according to a distinctive code of ethics that continually evolved over time and was flavored by various regional peculiarities. The samurai's canon is commonly referred as Bushido, literally "the way of the warrior." It became one of the first internationally recognized Japanese words over a century ago, with the publication in English of Nitobe Inazo's *Bushido: The Soul of Japan* (1899). A bestseller to this day, Nitobe's book attempts to explain the well-ordered ethos of the samurai as being centered on the seven virtues of rectitude, courage, benevolence, respect, sincerity, honor, and loyalty. It is upon Nitobe's thesis that most people in Japan and abroad now glean their understanding of the samurai mindset. The reality of their existence, however, was far more multifaceted and complex than the prevailing depictions of the samurai, namely as paragons of traditional morality and all that is majestic, suggest.

Instead of dry scholarly accounts, mainstream understanding of the samurai is influenced predominantly by novels, manga, anime, and movies. Ironically, even academic discourse on the samurai is, to a greater or lesser extent, unwittingly inspired by these renditions from popular culture. As was the case centuries ago when samurai actually existed, the line between fact and fiction remains a very hazy one indeed.

Gavin Blair's latest book is a wonderfully eye-catching addition to the body of work that seeks to identify misnomers, and provide the fundamental facts needed to make sense of the samurai legacy. As the old Japanese proverb "*Kagi no ana kara ten wo nozoku*" goes, from a gap as small as a keyhole one thinks one is looking at something as vast as the heavens. In contrast to that, this splendid volume portrays the vast experience of samurai culture—from their tools, important historical events, representative individuals, and female counterparts, through to their famous portrayals in popular culture—allowing the reader to hone in on reliable truths to facilitate an understanding of what made the samurai tick. The reader's interest will undoubtedly be piqued to investigate further, and so this book is the perfect introduction into the simultaneously chaotic but aesthetically sublime realm of samurai existence.

—Alex Bennett Ph.D.

ABOVE **Minamoto no Yorimitsu (948–1021), also known as Minamoto no Raiko, a renowned warrior of his clan, pictured here with a kite adorned with a demon.**

魚屋 北渓 **Totoya Hokkei (1780–1850)**

FRONT ENDPAPERS **Minamoto no Tametomo (1139–1170), a samurai famed for his archery prowess, being rescued by *tengu* demons sent by the retired Emperor Sutoku (1119–1164).**

歌川 国芳 **Utagawa Kuniyoshi (1798-1861)**

PAGE 1 **A well-preserved set of full samurai armor dating from 1662, known as *tosei gusoku* or full modern armor, with a breastplate (*do*) made of iron, gauntlets and sleeves, partly in response to the introduction of firearms to the battlefield. The breastplate is adorned with an image of the fearsome Buddhist deity Fudo Myoo (Acala), who was worshipped as a defender of the nation, and two of his acolytes.**

当世具足 *Tosei gusoku*

PAGES 2/3 **Kusunoki Masatsura (1326–1348), son of Masashige, at the Battle of Shijonawate, where he committed seppuku, portrayed by kabuki actor Ichikawa Danjuro IX.**

歌川 国芳 **Utagawa Kuniyoshi (1798-1861)**

CHAPTER 1

ORIGINS OF THE SAMURAI:
THE RISE OF A WARRIOR CLASS

Many warriors from the annals of the history of warfare have captured the imagination, but as a group, few to the extent that the samurai have. The reasons for this are many. Originating in the early Heian period (794–1185), when they had yet to acquire the moniker of samurai, they would exist for nearly a thousand years until the mid-19th century, ruling Japan in some form or other for almost 700 years. Famed for their katana swords and fierce loyalty, they were in reality more often mounted archers who could be treacherous when it was expedient.

The samurai—or *bushi*, as they are often referred to in Japan—were undoubtedly some of the most formidable fighting men, and not a few women, to have graced a battlefield. Though they sometimes strayed far from the semi-mythical Bushido code of honor, they were a fascinating cadre who were at the center of events during some of the most dramatic periods of history.

This book attempts to tell some of the pivotal stories of the samurai, explore the legends, detail their weaponry and warfare, describe what they did during peacetime, evaluate their influence on modern Japan, and dispel a few myths surrounding these legendary warriors. Names are presented in Japanese order: family names first. Many samurai went by multiple names, used concurrently on occasions, so here their most familiar are used.

The history of the human habitation of Japan is evidenced by the existence of simple tools used by hunter-gatherers dated to 40,000 years ago, around the time the archipelago became cut off from the Eurasian landmass. During the Jomon period (14,000 BC to 1,000 BC) the early people of Japan had begun to make "cord-marked" pottery, for which the era is named, some of the oldest known in the world.

The subsequent Yayoi period (1,000 BC to 250 AD) saw an influx of people (the Yayoi) from the Asian mainland who mixed with the existing population and brought with them a number of innovations. These included the development of systematic rice agriculture, a seminal moment in the history of the islands; a greater use of metals, woodwork, glass-making, and the emergence of social structures. Numerous powerful tribes and kingdoms were formed, the population grew to millions of people and the existence of Japanese civilization was recorded in Chinese historical texts of the time.

The Kofun period (250–538), named for the large, distinctive keyhole-shaped burial mounds of the era's aristocrats, saw much of Kyushu and the main Honshu island unified into a single state. The Yamato clan, from what is today's Kansai region (Kyoto,

Osaka and Kobe), came to dominate and its rulers became emperors whose line continues uninterrupted to this day, making it the world's longest surviving reigning dynasty.

SHOTOKU TAISHI 聖徳太子

The Asuka period (538–710) was defined by the arrival of Buddhism via the Korean kingdom of Baekje. The new religion found favor with the Soga clan that had recently risen to dominance and it was Shotoku Taishi, the prince regent for Empress Suiko, who was instrumental in its promotion. In the 660s, Emperor Tenji sent a huge expeditionary force to Baekje, something his mother Empress Saimei had begun preparations for before her death, to support Japan's ally against the combined armies of the Silla kingdom of Korea and Tang China. Japan's forces were crushed at the Battle of Hakusukinoe, resulting in the end of the young nation's direct involvement with continental Asia and the acceleration of shifts that would eventually lead to the emergence of the samurai.

The Taika Reforms implemented over decades in the seventh century were a series of measures designed to strengthen the control of the imperial government over its subjects. They were based on the Chinese governmental system and scholars were sent to the

Minamoto no Yorimitsu with his four senior retainers, known as the Four Heavenly Kings, killing the demon Shutendoji, one of the many legends the warrior appears in.

勝川 春亭 Katsukawa Shuntei (松高斎 Shokosai, 1770–1824)

Middle Kingdom to learn all they could from Asia's most advanced civilization. This huge importation of knowledge and culture would go on to shape Japan in ways that can still be felt today. The measures included a census and standing army raised by conscription.

Officers in the new system were assigned to one of 12 ranks, which were further subdivided, and those in the lower half were known as samurai, though they were responsible for relatively mundane administrative tasks. The origin of the term stems from the verb *saburau* or *samurau*, meaning to serve by someone's side. But it was not for another couple of centuries that the term would be used to describe the professional warriors who eventually became renowned around the globe. In Japanese, they are more frequently referred to as *bushi*, literally martial person and linked with the term Bushido, "the way of the warrior," the code which they are purported to have lived by. The word *buke*, meaning warrior family or house, is also commonplace.

ABOVE **In these two prints belonging to a triptych by Utagawa Yoshitsuya, Minamoto no Yorimitsu (948-1021) fights the demon Shutendoji on Mount Oe near Kyoto.**

歌川 芳艶 **Utagawa Yoshitsuya (1822–1866)**

OPPOSITE **A young Prince Shotoku 聖徳太子 (574–622) shown holding an incense burner, thought to be praying for his sick father, with two court attendants. The prince was instrumental in the establishment of Buddhism in Japan.**

A fully codified tax system was introduced as part of land reforms, which resulted in many small farms being swallowed up by large estates and the creation of a feudal system under wealthy landowners. These estates, known as *shoen*, became both fiscally and legally autonomous, which led to a weakening of the imperial government. The newly enriched and empowered lords began to employ soldiers to protect their lands and families, as well as fight rivals. It was the descendants of these men who would eventually become the samurai.

The government was still conscripting soldiers as it expected a revenge attack for its failed exploits on the Korean Peninsula. Garrisons were posted on the islands of Iki and Tsushima, which lay between Japan and Korea, and defenses were built around Hakata Bay in Kyushu. The attack would not come for another six centuries, at which time it was led by the Mongols, who were by then in control of much of both Korea and China.

As the immediate perceived threat from China receded, the Imperial Court rescinded the conscription law and hired private armies of warriors from the regions as necessary. The main military need from the early eighth to the early ninth century was in battling the Emishi people of the northeastern regions of the Honshu main island as the Yamato nation expanded in that direction. There is debate among historians and anthropologists over whether or not the Emishi were an ethnically separate group from the aboriginal Ainu of Hokkaido. Either way, they were a bearded, hairy people known for their tattoos. Combat experience against the Emishi played a significant role in shaping the samurai warrior.

The regions around the seat of imperial power on the Kinai region in the west (modern day Kansai) were by this time largely peaceful, and martial skills there were in decline. It was the fighting men of the Kanto plain to the east (where the modern city of Tokyo is located) whose prowess became renowned. The courtiers of the west began to devote more time, when they were not engaged in political intriguing, to artistic and cultural pursuits, looking down on their uncouth country cousins in the east. It is easy to imagine what the warriors of the east thought of the effete nobles of the west. Vestiges of this Kinai-Kanto rivalry are still apparent in contemporary Japan, with some residents of each region maintaining negative stereotypical images of the other.

It was the ongoing campaigns against the Emishi, culminating in the Thirty-Eight Years' War of 774–811, which kept the Kanto warriors battle-hardened. And the term shogun has its origins in these conflicts: the leaders of the Japanese forces were given the title *seii taishogun*, meaning the general who subdues the barbarians of the east.

Combat against the hairy barbarians also wrought changes to the way Japanese warriors fought. The Emishi were known as skilled horseback archers who used asymmetric bows and then curved swords to cut down riders at closer quarters. The Japanese armies adopted these tactics and weapons, likely

propelled by Emishi soldiers who joined their ranks either through subjugation or alliances. Horseback archery became the military mainstay of the samurai. They also used swords which eventually evolved into the legendary katana.

The ranks of the newly professionalized soldiers included a growing cadre of disinherited imperial offspring who would go on to form some of the most notable samurai clans or houses. The reason this legion of former princes and princesses existed is that all children sired by the emperor, whether born to wives, concubines or other women, were considered legitimate and therefore had potential claims to the throne. In an effort to reduce both the potential for such successional confusion and the financial burden

LEFT This series of three scrolls from the 14th century known as *Illustrated Biography of Prince Shotoku* were commissioned by the Sumiyoshi clan, who acted as patrons to generations of painters. Here the prince is shown flying over Mt. Fuji on his horse, one of many legends surrounding him was that he was able to disappear into the clouds and travel around Japan in this manner.

聖徳太子絵伝＿第二幅 *Illustrated Biography of Prince Shotoku, section 2.*

ABOVE Episodes from Shotoku's life in his twenties, when he had already been appointed Prince Regent, are depicted here. He helped build a centralized government around the emperor on Confucian principles, as well as propagate Buddhism in Japan through building temples such as Horyu-ji in Nara.

聖徳太子絵伝＿第三幅 *Illustrated Biography of Prince Shotoku, section 3.*

LEFT Scenes from the court, where Shotoku effectively ruled in place of his aunt Empress Suiko, along with Soga no Umako. Another legend is that Shotoku could listen to multiple conversations at once. Also known has Prince Umayado, he is revered in Japan to this day and has appeared on a number of banknotes.

聖徳太子絵伝＿第一幅 *Illustrated Biography of Prince Shotoku, section 1.*

ABOVE The prince was responsible for the Seventeen Article Constitution, Japan's first, which enshrined the power of emperors and empresses, even though he wielded much of the real power during his reign.

聖徳太子絵伝＿第一幅 *Illustrated Biography of Prince Shotoku, section 1.*

16

RIGHT **Emperor Saga** 嵯峨天皇
(786–842) ruled as the 52nd
emperor from 809–823 and
fathered so many children that
his estranged offspring formed
two powerful clans which
became bloody rivals for the
right to rule Japan.

of the burgeoning royal household, some of the imperial progeny were forced to leave, often granted land and given new family names.

The Emperor Saga, who ruled in the early ninth century, was a particularly prolific potentate, fathering more than 50 children by at least 30 women. Saga had 32 of his huge litter pushed out of the court. Two such clans were the Taira and the Minamoto. They would go on to fight each other for control of the nation in bitter, prolonged conflicts.

Whether of noble birth or not, soldiers hired by the nobles were exempt from taxation, adding an obvious attraction to the profession. These factors combined to create the environment from which the samurai would be forged into a warrior class, raising their children in the martial ways and seeing themselves first and foremost as professional soldiers who accepted death as part of life. It would not however be until the 16th century that the samurai would be legally codified as a fixed caste, ironically by a warlord who had risen to rule the nation after being born into a peasant family.

BELOW **Part of a scroll by Tosa Mitsunobu 土佐光信 (1434–1525), it is the only surviving picture of the campaign against the tribes of the Emishi people of the north by Sakanoue no Tamuramaro (758–811), one of the first generals to be given the title** *seii taishogun* **(barbarian-subduing generalissimo); the title shogun was later adopted by the samurai rulers of the nation.**

紙本著色清水寺縁起 *Illustrated Scroll of Legends about the Origin of Kiyomizu-dera Temple*

CHAPTER 2

BATTLE OF THE CLANS:
THE TAIRA AND THE MINAMOTO

Of the samurai clans which grew out of the branches of the imperial family cut loose from court, the Taira and Minamoto grew to be the most powerful. Not only did the sons marry other nobles, but their houses' names rang out so strongly that many men who married Taira and Minamoto daughters took on their family name.

It was a dispute over a marriage between two nobles that eventually led to one of the most dramatic rebellions and challenges to imperial power of the time. Somewhat curiously, both parties were of the Taira clan, so their names would have remained unchanged. Warlord Taira no Masakado was set to marry his cousin but refused to acquiesce to her father's demand that Masakado join his family and live with them. Both the slighted father Taira no Yoshikane, who saw his prospective son-in-law as below him in the aristocratic pecking order, and the fiery Masakado brought respective allies, including a Minamoto warlord, into the conflict, which soon escalated into open warfare. Masakado would be victorious, but despite sparing his adversary's life, he was censured by the imperial court for torching villages during their battles. Trouble later flared again and took a new twist when in 939, after attacking an imperial outpost in Hitachi, in today's Ibaraki Prefecture, and taking control of a number of local provinces, he declared himself *shinno* or new emperor of Kanto.

TAIRA NO MASAKADO 平 将門

Masakado's demise came the following year after the imperial court had responded to the threat to their authority by putting a price on his head and sending an army to take it. His army was defeated and Masakado killed, his head cut off and taken to Kyoto. Legend has it that his skull's final resting place was in what is now Tokyo and it is said to be protected by a curse that some are still fearful of to this day.

Masakado became mythologized and stories of him, some that portray him as a giant born of a snake and with skin that was impervious to wounds, would

RIGHT **Taira no Masakado 平 将門, a ruthless warlord from the early 10th century not averse to disposing of his own relatives, overreached by declaring himself *shinno* or new emperor, leading to his downfall. His head was taken by his cousin Taira no Sadamori, whose father he had killed, at the Battle of Kojima in 940. From the series *Mirror of Famous Generals of Our Country*.**

歌川 芳員 **Utagawa Yoshikazu (active 1848–1870)**

本朝名将鏡

平親王将門

金五

一寿齋
芳員画

be told for centuries. More grounded in reality is the fact that his conflicts were some of the earliest massed warrior-on-warrior battles. He is reputed to be the first samurai to call out his family name and lineage as he commenced battle, a tradition which would be adopted by many *bushi* in the subsequent bloody centuries.

One of those who fought in the campaign against Masakado was Minamoto no Tsunemoto, who a year later in 941, helped defeat a pirate fleet of "more than a thousand boats" led by Fujiwara Sumitomo. He terrorized ships in the Inland Sea, a body of water vital to trade. Sumitomo had been sent to the region to subdue the watery brigands, but instead installed himself as their leader. Sumitomo hailed from a branch of the Fujiwara clan which had fallen on hard times, while another branch maintained its stranglehold over the court by intermarrying with the imperial family and providing most of the regents for emperors. Fujiwara's power began to decline, but from the 10th to the 12th centuries, they and the Taira and Minamoto would wrestle for control of the court, territories, and alliances with other clans. Many of the branch families were closely related to each other and disputes often crossed clan lines, with kinfolk going into battle against their own. Cousins or even brothers fought each other as alliances shifted and treachery abounded.

LEFT **A portrait of Minamoto no Yoritomo 源 頼朝 (1147–1199), who was a descendant of Emperor Seiwa and became the first true shogun ruler in 1192 after protracted and bloody conflict with the rival Taira clan. Despite wielding almost absolute power as shogun, Yoritomo remained suspicious and jealous of his half-brother Yoshitsune and had him hunted down. The artist, date and whether it is truly a depiction of Yoritomo have all been disputed.**

One such war was the Hogen Rebellion of 1156, which saw all three families lined up on both sides. The conflict was over the Fujiwara's influence on imperial succession, and the battles were fought in the capital itself. Taira no Kiyomori and Minamoto no Yoshitomo, the heads of their respective clans, actually fought on the same victorious side of Emperor Go-Shirakawa, establishing them as the pre-eminent families in court. In the aftermath, complex machinations in the jostling for power between the two clans continued. Just three years later, another dispute over the imperial throne brought war once more to the streets of Kyoto.

The Heiji Insurrection (1160) saw clearer clan demarcation, with the red banners of the Taira standing against the white of the Minamoto, though the ever-flexible Fujiwara fought on both sides. When Kiyomori took a month-long religious pilgrimage, the Minamoto saw a window of opportunity to attack the imperial residence. He made captives of the teenage Emperor Nijo and his father, the retired Emperor Go-Shirakawa and still wielder of power through his position as regent. Hearing of the grab for power in Kyoto, Kiyomori gathered hundreds of Taira loyalists on his way back to the city but feigned a plea of peace on his return. The events of the insurrection also became of the stuff of legend, particularly the escape of Emperor Nijo disguised as a woman, and his father dressed as a member of the imperial staff, aided by Taira agents. Following further shrewd strategizing by Kiyomori, the Minamoto were defeated, Yoshitomo and his two eldest sons executed. There are various theories explaining what prompted Kiyomori to exile rather than kill Yoshitomo's three remaining sons. Perhaps it was Kiyomori's stepmother who persuaded the victorious clan leader to spare the three on condition they were banished to monasteries. Kiyomori's mercy would come back to haunt him when the trio, Yoritomo,

Yoshitsune and Noriyori, grew up to be powerful samurai who would wreak vengeance on the Taira.

Minamoto no Yoshitsune was in many ways the archetypal samurai: a skilled warrior, he was known as fiercely loyal and chivalrous towards women. Myth has it that he was trained to fight with the sword and war-fan by *tengu*, fantastical goblin-like creatures, at night on the mountainsides around the Kurama-dera temple to which he had been exiled. According to popular accounts, Yoshitsune would later happen upon a bear of a man known as Benkei, who had been too much of a handful for the warrior-monks at the Enryaku-ji temple and expelled. The story goes that they met on Gojo Bridge, where Benkei had been adding to his collection of swords by defeating their owners. Having reached 999, Benkei was looking forward to making it a round thousand when he spied the young Yoshitsune approaching. After a master class in swordsmanship from the young Minamoto, Benkei swore allegiance to him and the two became inseparable.

In 1180 began the Genpei War between the Taira and the Minamoto, though it is more accurately described as a number of significant battles and a series of smaller skirmishes. It brought the brothers Yoritomo and Yoshitsune together for the first time since their childhood. The Battle of Uji, at an important crossing of a river into Kyoto, was the opening salvo, giving first blood to the Taira. The battle is also famous in the war tales for Minamoto no Yorimasa's seppuku after his defeat, one of the earliest cases of a fully ritualized stomach cutting by a samurai.

Fighting continued across the west of Japan in the following years and the tide began to turn for the Minamoto. By 1184, Yoshitsune had been appointed general of the Minamoto forces, and he won famous victories alongside his brother Noriyori at the second Battle of Uji and at Ichi-no-Tani. The decisive blow

was struck at the 1185 naval Battle of Dan-no-ura, where most of the remaining Taira clan and the child Emperor Antoku perished. So many died in the narrow straits between Honshu and Kyushu that some believe the *heike* crabs from the waterway are still inhabited by the spirits of the Taira samurai, with the occasional specimen found with what appears to be a face on its shell only adding to the myth.

Yoshitsune initially escaped with the help of the trusty Benkei, a tale that entered Japanese folklore, but eventually committed seppuku as men working for Yoritomo closed in on him.

In 1192, Yoritomo declared himself *seii taishogun*, literally barbarian-subduing generalissimo, and established the first warrior-led government of Japan. Sakanoue no Tamuramaro (758–811) was given the title centuries beforehand, but never wielded authority like Yoritomo.

The Kamakura shogunate would last until 1333, when the Emperor Go-Daigo revolted and restored imperial rule for just three years in the Kenmu Restoration. He was overthrown by Ashikaga Takauji who then went on to form the second of Japan's three shogunates. The Ashikaga shogunate lasted until 1573, however, as with the Kamakura period, the shogun's authority was actually nominal.

Two of Japan's most famous warlords, Oda Nobunaga and Toyotomi Hideyoshi, did not assume the shogun title, although they were destined to become the most powerful men in the country. After the inroads they made in unifying the country, it was Tokugawa Ieyasu who finally did become shogun in 1603 when he started the third shogunate. The Tokugawa regime ruled until the Meiji Restoration in 1868, when Tokugawa Yoshinobu, the 15th Tokugawa shogun, abdicated to mark the end of the samurai era. Japan had been under shogun rule, to some extent or other, for six and a half centuries.

Minamoto no Yorimasa 源 頼政 (1106–1180), a general, poet and sometime Buddhist priest. His death at the Battle of Uji, near Kyoto, after defeat by the armies of the Taira clan, was one of the first recorded incidents of ritual suicide by a samurai. Yorimasa briefly allied himself with the Taira, before returning to the fold.

LEFT This image from the same screen shows the Battle of Heiji (Heiji Insurrection) of 1160, which was fought between the Minamoto and the Taira on the streets of Kyoto, causing destruction in the ancient city and terrorizing its citizenry. The Taira were victorious in the battle, though they would ultimately lose the war.

保元平治合戦図屏風 *The Rebellions of the Hogen and Heiji Eras* folding screen

ABOVE Part of a painted screen titled *The Rebellions of the Hogen and Heiji Eras*, which shows two civil wars, the Hogen Rebellion in the summer of 1156 and Heiji Rebellion in early 1160, in a single tableau detailing the two conflicts that would lead to decades of a bloody Taira-Minamoto civil war.

保元平治合戦図屏風 *The Rebellions of the Hogen and Heiji Eras* folding screen

Warriors from the Taira, Minamoto and Fujiwara clans actually fought on both sides during the Hogen Rebellion, but by the Heiji battles, the Taira and Minamoto were mostly pitted against each other. This detail from the top of *The Rebellions of the Hogen and Heiji Eras* screen painting shows mounted samurai and foot soldiers fighting, with what may be Lake Biwa, or the Uji River which flows from it, in the background.

保元平治合戦図屏風 *The Rebellions of the Hogen and Heiji Eras* folding screen

In this detail from the screen painting what appear to be Taira samurai, judging by the red banner, are overrunning a residence of a Minamoto samurai, who is committing ritual suicide by cutting his stomach open. The red of the Taira and white of the Minamoto make up the colors of the modern Japanese flag.

保元平治合戦図屏風 *The Rebellions of the Hogen and Heiji Eras* folding screen

BELOW Taira no Atsumori 平敦盛 and Kumagai no Jiro Naozane 熊谷次郎直実 square up at the Battle of Ichi-no-tani (1184), one of the crucial battles of the Genpei War. Kumagai killed Atsumori and the Taira were defeated. The duel between the two, which became famous as Kumagai was reluctant to take the head of the young Atsumori who reminded him of his own son, became a staple of books and plays. Minamoto no Yoshitsune and his warrior monk attendant Benkei also fought alongside each other at the battle.

歌川国貞 Utagawa Kunisada (三代歌川豊国 Utagawa Toyokuni III, 1786–1865)

RIGHT The naval Battle of Dan-no-ura fought in the Straits of Shimonoseki between the main island of Honshu and Kyushu (1185) was the last stand of the Taira clan, victory handed power to the Minamoto and brought the Genpei War to a close. Around 750 ships participated in the battle and casualties included the six-year-old Emperor Antoku, along with most of the Taira clan.

壇ノ浦の戦い Battle of Dan-no-ura

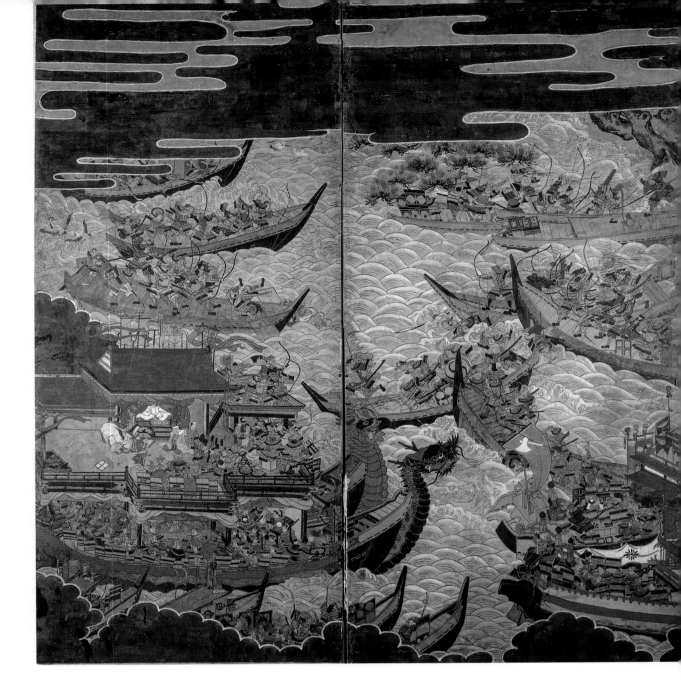

PAGES 30–33 A screen painting from the early 17th century inspired by the *Tale of Heike* 平家物語 (*Heike Monogatari*), an epic account of the Genpei War thought to have been written in the early 13th century and based on oral stories of the conflicts. The *Heike* referred to the Taira clan, while the Minamoto were also known as Genji. The Genpei War established the samurai as rulers of Japan for the next six and a half centuries.

源平合戦 Genpei War

CHAPTER 3

SAMURAI VERSUS THE MONGOLS:
THE KAMIKAZE "DIVINE WIND"

The early decades of the 13th century had seen the former Emperor Go-Toba attempt unsuccessfully to wrest back power from the Kamakura shogunate's Hojo regents, ending in a major battle at Uji, near Kyoto in 1221. This was followed in 1229 by the Kangi Famine, almost certainly one of the worst in the nation's history, which over three years decimated the population. It led to societal breakdown and even drove raiding parties to the Korean Peninsula in search of food. Less than half a century later, a far larger and more dangerous raiding party would come from the opposite direction.

The intervening period was relatively calm as Japan struggled to recover, but this did not put a stop to the political intriguing between the Court and the shogunate, or rivalry between samurai clans. As has often been the case throughout human history, it took an overwhelming outside threat to bring about some semblance of unity.

Kublai Khan, grandson of Genghis, had risen to the throne of the then fragmenting Mongol Empire in 1260, and was already looking across the water before he established the Yuan Dynasty by subduing northern China. Kublai sent emissaries to the "king" of Japan gently suggesting it become a vassal state of his empire. A surviving letter from Kublai displays an uncharacteristically conciliatory tone, by Mongol standards, ending: "Hence we dispatched a mission with our letter particularly expressing our wishes. Enter into friendly relations with each other from now on. We think all countries belong to one family. How are we in the right, unless we comprehend this?

Nobody would wish to resort to arms."

The shogunate, led by the young regent Hojo Tokimune, ignored the dovish counsel of the Imperial Court and ignored the Khan. Tokimune ordered samurai from the clans of Kyushu to return to their homelands and prepare to defend against invasion, while also assembling a reinforcing army.

RIGHT **Images from the attempted Mongol invasions, in 1274 and 1281, from a set of scrolls known as** *Moko Shurai Ekotoba* **or** *Illustrated Account of the Mongol Invasion.* **The top image shows samurai rowing out to attack the Mongol fleet, probably during the Battle of Koan in 1281. The third image shows samurai of the Shoni clan gathering to defend the homeland in the first invasion in 1274. The man admiring the horse in the bottom image is Takezaki Suenaga (outside the residence of Lord Adachi) who had the scrolls made to detail his brave deeds, in the hope of being rewarded by the shogunate.**

蒙古襲来絵詞 *Illustrated Account of the Mongol Invasion*

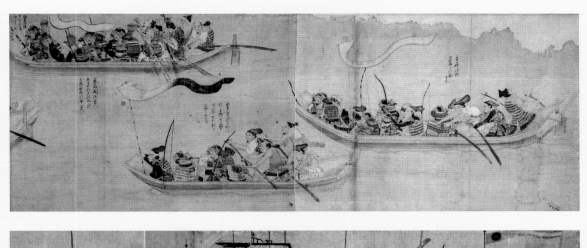

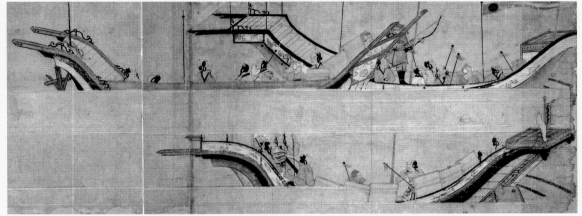

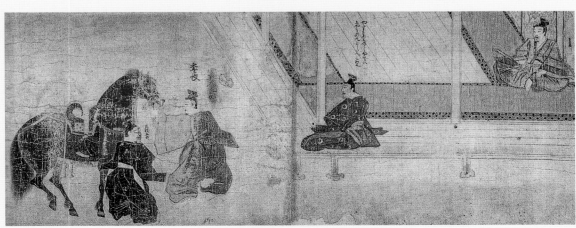

In October 1274, a fleet left recently subjugated Korea carrying between 20,000 and 40,000 Mongol, Chinese and Koreans heading for Kyushu. The expeditionary force made short work of a small samurai garrison on Tsushima Island led by So Sukekuni, a descendant of the mostly vanquished Taira clan. After massacring much of Tsushima's citizenry, and allegedly fastening captured women to the front of their ships as human shields, the fleet sailed for the smaller island of Iki, where the defenders and citizens befell a similar fate.

Arriving in Hakata Bay, near today's Fukuoka, in early November, a few thousand samurai awaited them. The samurai apparently did not heed the warnings of survivors of the island battles and individual warriors were recorded in chronicles as riding onto the beaches and proclaimed their names and lineage to the incoming invaders, expecting honorable one-on-one combat. They were met with hails of poisoned arrows and units advancing in forma-tion under metal shields, along with explosive devices launched by catapults. After a day of fierce fighting, the samurai withdrew to centuries-old fortifications, while the invaders regrouped on their fleet. The defenders believed reinforcements offered their only hope.

Meanwhile, the Mongol forces were apparently surprised at the strength of the samurai's resistance, which included a lucky piece of archery that had badly wounded a Korean general. They were also concerned about their own diminished stock of arrows.

Overnight, the Japanese launched a surprise counter-attack, sneaking up on the fleet in hundreds of small boats, some of which were employed as fire-ships. After archers took out sentries on some of the ships, samurai boarded them, wreaking havoc among the unprepared troops and sailors. Other ships were set ablaze by the floating incendiary vessels, making their crews easy targets for samurai archers. As a storm began to brew, the samurai rowed back to shore, while the Mongol fleet was ravaged, sinking some ships, beaching others, killing more than 10,000 of the invaders, according to some records.

The shogunate correctly assumed this would not be the last they heard of the Mongols and Kublai sent further diplomatic missions, some of whom were not allowed to land in Japan, and all of whom returned bearing no reply. One group of five were told not to leave without an answer and resolved to stay in the bakufu capital Kamakura until they got one. Tokimune had them executed.

This depiction of Mongol soldiers was probably copied from the original scrolls. The original artist, who would have created the scrolls shortly after the Mongol attacks, because Takezaki Suenaga, a samurai from Kyushu, had them made to claim his spoils from the shogunate, is unknown.

蒙古襲来絵詞 *Illustrated Account of the Mongol Invasion*

Having brought southern China under the Khanate, Kublai ordered a much larger invasion force to be assembled. In 1281, a fleet carrying 25,000 troops left Korea and a larger fleet from China with more than 100,000 soldiers was to rendezvous with it at Iki Island. Marco Polo wrote of seeing the improbably large number of 15,000 vessels on the Yangzi River, but including the tens of thousands of sailors, this armada was likely the largest seaborne assault in history until the D-Day landings of 1944.

This painting shows samurai who fought against the Mongols during the invasions. The bakufu shogunate government expected Kublai Khan's forces of Mongols, Chinese and Koreans to attempt another invasion, but it never came.

The samurai clans had spent the intervening years building defensive walls along Hakata Bay, the only place where a fleet the size of the Mongol's could land, and had as many as 40,000 men ready to fight.

Although the resistance on Tsushima and Iki was fiercer this time, the final result was the same. After becoming impatient with a delay in the departure of the Chinese fleet, the smaller force from Korea sailed ahead into Hakata Bay. There followed five weeks of back-and-forth, with the invaders trying to land and the samurai again employing guerrilla raids with small boats and fire-ships. The line of the newly-built walls held fast and there were also traditional land battles on an island in the bay which the Mongol forces had used to quarter their horses. When the armada from China arrived, it sensibly bypassed Hakata, dropping anchor a day's ride south and sent troops ashore to battle the samurai armies through villages along the coast.

Much of the huge combined army of Mongol, Chinese and Korean troops stayed aboard the fleet of ships, which was chained together and surrounded by wooden walkways. The Mongols appeared not to have learned the lessons of their first foray, and alongside the warships, the fleet included troop transports of poor quality, hastily repaired old vessels and flat-bottomed Chinese river craft. When a storm

far larger than what had struck seven years earlier whipped up in mid-August, the invasion fleet was devastated. Whether the fleet was already in retreat when the storm began, along with how many tens of thousands perished, is disputed by historians.

What is beyond doubt is that an unusually powerful storm played a part in the destruction of the invasion fleet. Nakaba Yamada's account *Ghenko: The Mongol Invasion of Japan*, published in 1916, described the fate of the vessels thus: "Heavily freighted with human beings and weighty weapons, they sank by hundreds. The corpses were piled on the shore, or floated on the water so thickly that it seemed almost possible to walk thereon. The fortified armada, with chains which connected each vessel, was totally wrecked and dashed to pieces."

Wrecks of ships from the Mongol fleet were discovered off the coast of Japan in 2011 and 2015, helping to confirm some of the accounts from the time.

During the battle, both the shogunate and the Imperial Court are said to have sent requests to shrines

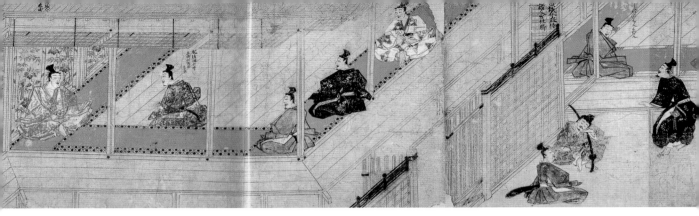

and temples to pray for the nation's salvation. The two storms were hailed as *shinpu* (divine wind), which confirmed to those inclined to believe as much that Japan was a sacred land protected by the gods.

Many centuries later, at the end of World War Two, the name would be given to the *shinpu toku-betsu kogeki tai* or divine wind special attack units of the Imperial Japanese Navy, which carried out suicide attacks on Allied ships. They were informally referred to as "kamikaze," an alternative reading of the same characters, the term by which they became known around the world.

Needless to say, various religious institutions were keen to take as much credit as possible for the divine intervention, with some priests claiming they were praying for a storm at the precise moment it began to blow. And it was not only temples and shrines looking to be rewarded for their efforts.

TOP Takezaki Suenaga staking his claim to heroism during the invasions to Adachi Yasumori, a senior vassal at the shogunate of Hojo Tokimune in Kamakura. Adachi was later accused of conspiring against the Hojo clan.

蒙古襲来絵詞 *Illustrated Account of the Mongol Invasion*

ABOVE The Battle of Torikai-Gata was a decisive victory in 1274 by samurai, led by Takezaki Suenaga, over the invaders, with 3,500 Mongolian casualties. This led the Mongol army to retreat by sea, where their fleet was battered by a storm that became known as the kamikaze (divine wind).

蒙古襲来絵詞 *Illustrated Account of the Mongol Invasion*

BELOW One of the successful attacks by the Japanese forces on the ships of the second Mongolian invasion in 1281. The defenders also used the tactics of sending fire ships into the Mongolian fleet at night, which caused both fires to spread across the wooden boats and panic among the invading forces. Takezaki Suenaga is again shown to be at the heart of the action, unsurprisingly since this was the purpose of these scrolls he had commissioned.

蒙古襲来絵詞 *Illustrated Account of the Mongol Invasion*

BOTTOM Samurai on the stone walls at Hakata Bay, near modern day Fukuoka, where they repelled a smaller Mongol force, which retreated to its ships. A lack of arrows is said to have hampered the invaders' efforts. The date is recorded as November 19, 1274.

蒙古襲来絵詞 *Illustrated Account of the Mongol Invasion*

One of the most important primary sources for the two invasions is a series of illustrated scrolls commissioned by a samurai called Takezaki Suenaga, who fought against the Mongols in 1274 and 1281. Although they were damaged, lost for centuries and even added to at later dates, they provide invaluable details of how events unfolded. The scrolls were ordered by Takezaki to provide proof of his heroic exploits to the shogunate, and he delivered them personally to Kamakura in an attempt to ensure he received adequate recompense. And therein lay a major problem for the bakufu. After the conflicts in which the samurai had for centuries fought, there was land, loot and titles taken from the vanquished that could be bestowed upon the loyal supporters of the victorious side. No such bounty was available after the Mongols had been repelled, resulting in a large contingent of disgruntled samurai clans unhappy with their reward for the sacrifices they had made in helping to save the nation. The financial strain of payments that were made to samurai and temples, along with the costs of garrisoning defenses against an expected third invasion, would go on to play a part in bringing about the demise of Hojo rule.

LEFT ABOVE **A horseback charge led by Takezaki Suenaga's brother-in-law routing a group of Mongol invaders, who can be seen on another section of the scroll, during the Battle of Torikai-Gata in 1274.**

蒙古襲来絵詞 *Illustrated Account of the Mongol Invasion*

LEFT BELOW **Takezaki Suenaga is seen aboard one of the boats the samurai used to attack the Mongol fleet anchored off the shore of Hakata Bay during the second invasion attempt by the forces of Kublai Khan, who was then ruler of the Yuan dynasty of China.**

蒙古襲来絵詞 *Illustrated Account of the Mongol Invasion*

BELOW **This scene from the second scroll shows Takezaki Suenaga reports his heroics from the second series of battles, with the heads of vanquished Mongols as proof, to Adachi Morimune, who had traveled from Kyushu to the shogunate in Kamakura. Morimune was the son of Adachi Yasumori, who Suenaga is seen telling of his exploits in the first scroll.**

蒙古襲来絵詞 *Illustrated Account of the Mongol Invasion*

CHAPTER 4

TOOLS OF THE TRADE:
SWORDS, BOWS, SPEARS, FIREARMS, CASTLES AND ARMOR

Although the samurai were known for engaging in cultural pursuits such as calligraphy, poetry and painting, while some became rulers, administrators and even accountants, they were of course at their core warriors. Their stock in trade was killing. Most associated with the katana, and commonly referred to as swordsmen, in reality the *bushi* used a range of weapons, and throughout much of their history blades were not even the primary tool for dispensing death. The iconic image of the samurai may be a one-on-one sword duel, but their battles were full of bows, spears, firearms in the later centuries, and castle sieges.

WEAPONS

The "sword is the soul of the warrior," said the shogun who unified Japan, Tokugawa Ieyasu. The katana certainly had special meaning for the samurai and is one of the most revered weapons in military history. The razor-sharp cutting edge and flexibility were achieved through a complex process of smelting the steel, repeated folding and then cooling the two parts of the blade with wet clay at different temperatures to create curvature. A lengthy, laborious polishing process further enhanced the curve and produced the gleaming sheen.

The wooden *tsuka* handle is wrapped in skin from a giant ray and then bound with cord. The *tsuba* guard and *saya* scabbards were often elaborately decorated, particularly in peacetime, creating what have become seen as works of fine art and collectors

pieces. Katana were paired with a simpler *wakizashi* short sword or a *tanto* dagger, the two blades denoting the bearer was a samurai.

The best swordsmiths became famous in their own right and their finest blades were sometimes presented to daimyo or shogun as gifts. A swordsmith known as Honjo Masamune, who worked during the late 13th and early 14th centuries, is widely regarded as the greatest ever exponent of his craft. His blades

RIGHT **A woodblock print shows Honjo Shigenaga (1540–1614), wielder of the legendary Honjo Masamune katana. Here he is blocking an exploding projectile with an iron shield at the Battle of Kawanakajima, after which he rebelled against his lord, Uesugi Kenshin. The artist was Utagawa Kuniyoshi, a master of the ukiyo-e style.**

歌川 国芳 **Utagawa Kuniyoshi (1798–1861)**

本庄越前守繁長

越前守繁長ハ謙信虎千代の幼年より補佐しつゝ
實か開國の元老ありさてハ彼大戦の又海津の押へ

西
余山の武
田勢
追々
川中嶋へ
帰着也
午の刻
川原面へ引返しさ敵将馬場信
房より打
出る鉄砲両よりあげく
先手の軍卒をさき繁長馬より
飛でおつ巳ゐ
づけとらの佐小兼て造せらる鉄の
櫓重さより難きのを軽じく
差るぎ煙の内を進行する
凡人の所為ならじと
人ミその舌をぞ巻ふりける

應需　柳下亭種員誌

過き濱より味方の箕色甚あつく
大将の来旗折懸中小澤み
さるを選小見て旗本を救ぎんハあつ危
一勇齋
國芳圖

This scene from a screen painting depicts bow
makers at work making *daikyu* longbows in the
16th century, during the Sengoku period, the
bloodiest period in samurai history. The samurai
longbow was made from laminated bamboo, other
woods and leather, a construction that remains
largely unchanged in today's *kyudo* archery.

大弓 *Daikyu*

were used by the Tokugawa clan, including the Honjo Masamune, a designated Japanese National Treasure which remains missing since it was reportedly handed to a member of the US occupying forces by a Tokugawa descendant when ownership of samurai swords was banned after World War Two. The 1876 Haitorei Edict, which stripped former samurai of the right to wear swords, was a symbolic declawing of their class that publicly brought down the curtain on their reign over Japan.

Armorers at work during the 16th century, from a screen painting. Styles of armor changed through the ages, becoming more decorative during times of relative peace. The origins of samurai armor were likely Chinese, like so much in Japan at the time, though it was adapted and evolved over the centuries. The basic structure was a series of overlapping plates constructed from iron and leather.

鎧 *Yoroi*

刀
KATANA
LONG SWORD

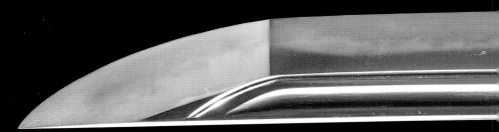

Detail of the *tang* or *nakago* (hilt) of the sword, with an inscription reading Asakura Kaoru Tekiri Tachiya—December 3rd year of Tensho, likely a later owner of the katana. The date corresponds to 1575 on the modern calendar. The sword may have been the work of Masamune of Sagami province, a legendary sword maker who forged katana in the late 13th and early 14th centuries.

相州正宗　Soshu Masamune of Sagami province
(ca. 1264–1343, attributed to)—刀 Long sword (katana)

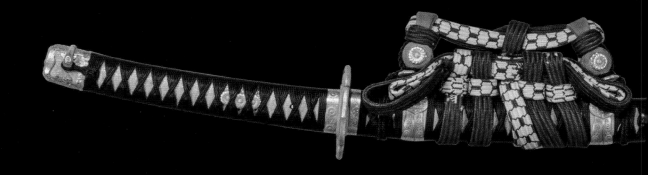

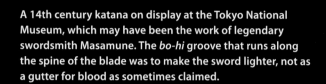

A 14th century katana on display at the Tokyo National Museum, which may have been the work of legendary swordsmith Masamune. The *bo-hi* groove that runs along the spine of the blade was to make the sword lighter, not as a gutter for blood as sometimes claimed.

相州正宗　Soshu Masamune of Sagami province
(ca. 1264–1343, attributed to)—刀 Long sword (katana)

梨地菊紋蒔絵螺鈿糸巻太刀

The scabbard of this 19th-century sword, housed in the Tokyo National Museum, is decorated with a pattern of chrysanthemums inlaid with the *raden* technique on *nashiji* lacquer, a name thought to allude to its resemblance to the dotted skin of the Japanese pear (nashi). It is a good example of the particularly rich styles characteristic of the Edo period, a relatively peaceful era.

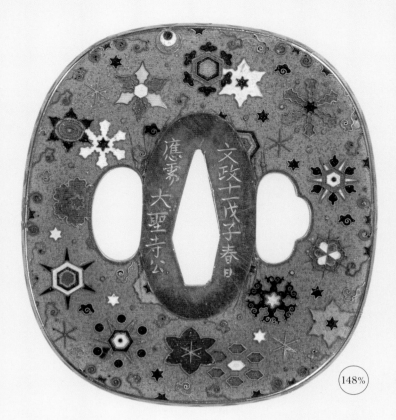

(148%)

鐔
TSUBA
HAND GUARDS

LEFT A *tsuba* (hand guard) from a katana features a snow flower cloisonné design. It is another example of aesthetics being as important, or more so, than practicality during the Edo period. The inscription dates the guard to 1828.

平田春寛 *Haruhiro Hirata school (19th century)*—雪華文七宝鐔 *Tsuba with snowflake design in cloisonné*

(130%)

LEFT This sword guard with a crane and clouds design is dated 1868, the first year of the Meiji era, just eight years before samurai would be forbidden from carrying katana. The name of the craftsman Goto Korai is also inscribed.

Goto Korai 後藤 光来 (1828–?)—雲鶴文鐔 *Tsuba with clouds and cranes design*

RIGHT A ukiyo-e woodblock print from 1848 by Utagawa Kuniyoshi of Oboshi Seizaemon Nobukiyo and Suto Senemon in the throes of a swordfight. From a series known as *Chushingishi komyo kurabe* (*Comparison of the High Renown of the Loyal Retainers and Faithful Samurai*).

歌川 国芳 Utagawa Kuniyoshi (1798–1861)

忠臣義士髙名競

須藤
仙右衛門

二八

大星
清左衛門信清

應需 一筆菴誌

一勇齋
國芳画

柄
TSUKA
HILTS

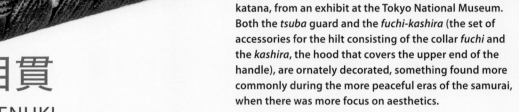

ABOVE Detail of a *tsuka* (hilt) hand grip from an Edo period katana, from an exhibit at the Tokyo National Museum. Both the *tsuba* guard and the *fuchi-kashira* (the set of accessories for the hilt consisting of the collar *fuchi* and the *kashira*, the hood that covers the upper end of the handle), are ornately decorated, something found more commonly during the more peaceful eras of the samurai, when there was more focus on aesthetics.

柄 *Tsuka*

目貫
MENUKI
ORNAMENTS

RIGHT A *menuki*, an ornament usually found under the cord wrapping on the handle of a katana that was designed to fit into the grip of the palm, in the form of a deer and an old turtle with seaweed growing from its back. This *menuki* is dated to the mid-19th century.

一壽 *Ichiju* (dates unknown)
—目貫 *Menuki*

(385%)

(372%)

LEFT A *menuki* from the late 18th or early 19th century in the shape of Idaten (Skanda), a Buddhist deity known for his speed, running with a reliquary (a container for sacred objects) on his head.

目貫 *Menuki*

RIGHT A woodblock print of kabuki actor Arashi Kichisaburo III in 1842 playing Kato Kiyomasa, a ruthless daimyo who served under Toyotomi Hideyoshi, one of the three unifiers of Japan.

歌川 国芳 Utagawa Kuniyoshi (1798–1861)

三所物
MITOKORO-MONO
ACCESSORIES

(142%)

(142%)

(250%)

Designs of catfish on algae on a *kogai*, a hairpin for samurai that was a form of katana accessory; a *menuki* palm grip handle ornament; and a *kozuka*, a handle for a small *kogatana* knife. From a 16th century sword.

後藤 乗真 Goto Joshin (1512–1562)—藻に鯰図三所物 Set of three kinds of sword fittings with catfish and seaweed

縁頭
FUCHIGASHIRA
HILT COLLAR AND POMMEL

A *fuchigashira*, matching fittings of hilt collar (*fuchi*) and pommel (*kashira*), the cap at the end of the handle, from an Edo period katana. *Fuchigashira* were designed to strengthen the handle, but were often decorated.

縁頭 *Fuchigashira*

(240%)

梨地水龍瑞雲文蒔絵宝剣（水龍剣）

NASHIJI MIZU RYU ZUIUNMON MAKIE HOKEN (MIZU RYU KEN)
WATER DRAGON SWORD WITH MAKI-E DESIGN OF WATER DRAGONS AND AUSPICIOUS CLOUDS

Details of a particularly ornate katana handle made by Kano Natsuo in 1873, in the very early years of the Meiji era as the age of the samurai was drawing to a close. It is likely the bearer of this sword never expected to draw it in anger, as evidenced by the lavish decoration of its *tsuka* (hilt) with a golden dragon.

Metal fittings: Kano Natsuo 加納 夏雄 (1828–1898)
柄 *Tsuka*

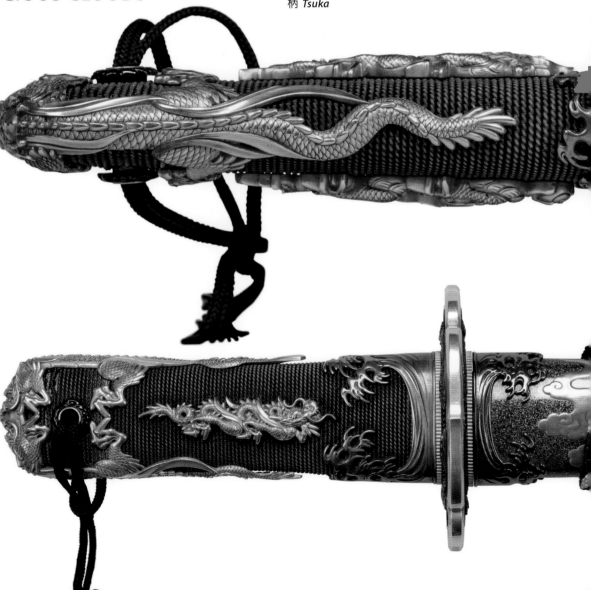

LEFT **Ghosts of defeated Taira clan warriors after the Battle of Dan-no-ura in a print *The Sea Bed at Daimotsu Bay* depicted in a woodblock print. Some of the Taira are portrayed as crabs, a reference to the enduring legend that the slain samurai were reborn in that form, as they prepare to attack Minamoto no Yoshitsune's ship.**

歌川 国芳 **Utagawa Kuniyoshi (1798–1861)**

弓 YUMI BOWS

An enduring feature of the Japanese longbow is its asymmetry, a characteristic identified from at least as far back as the seventh century, and still found in the bows used in the martial art of *kyudo* today. The grip is situated approximately a third of the way up the bow, which stand around six and half feet (two meters) tall. This has been ascribed to the use in early bows of a single young tree, which would be more flexible at the top. An asymmetrical design also made it easier for mounted archers to clear their horses with the bow when loosing arrows. By the time of mounted samurai archers, the bows were made by laminating bamboo and leather onto wood, with bowstrings of hemp coated with wax.

The earliest references to *bushi* in historical texts made no mention of swords, and warriors were known for their skills in *kyuba no michi*, the way of the horse and bow. The most prized samurai were ace mounted marksmen and later the armies of low-ranking *ashigaru* foot soldiers that fought in their armies were also populated by archers.

The art of the bow was so highly regarded that in the displays of ritualistic etiquette that preceded many samurai battles, archers from each side would shoot *kabura-ya* arrows with bulbous heads which hummed as they flew through the air. This signified the start of battle. Samurai trained in mounted archery contests known as *yabusame*. This was a practice introduced by the first shogun Minamoto no Yoritomo, who was concerned with the decline in horseback marksmanship among his samurai. *Yabusame* can still be seen at festivals in Japan today, and just how difficult it is to hit a target from a moving horse is evident.

One of the most celebrated samurai archers was Minamoto no Tametomo, who legend has it was able to draw a bow further back than usually possible because his left arm was much longer than his right. He was said to have sunk a ship of the rival Taira clan with a single arrow which punctured its hull. After he fought against Taira and Minamoto forces in a rebellion, his captors cut the tendons in his left arm, rendering him unable to pull a bow. He is the first samurai named in historical records to have committed seppuku.

RIGHT **A woodblock by Utagawa Toyokuni of actor Iwai Shijaku in the 1830s playing the young Taira no Atsumori (1169–1184), whose death at the hands of Kumagai no Jiro Naozane at the Battle of Ichi-no-Tani became the subject of numerous plays and stories.**

歌川 豊国 **Utagawa Toyokuni (1769–1825)**

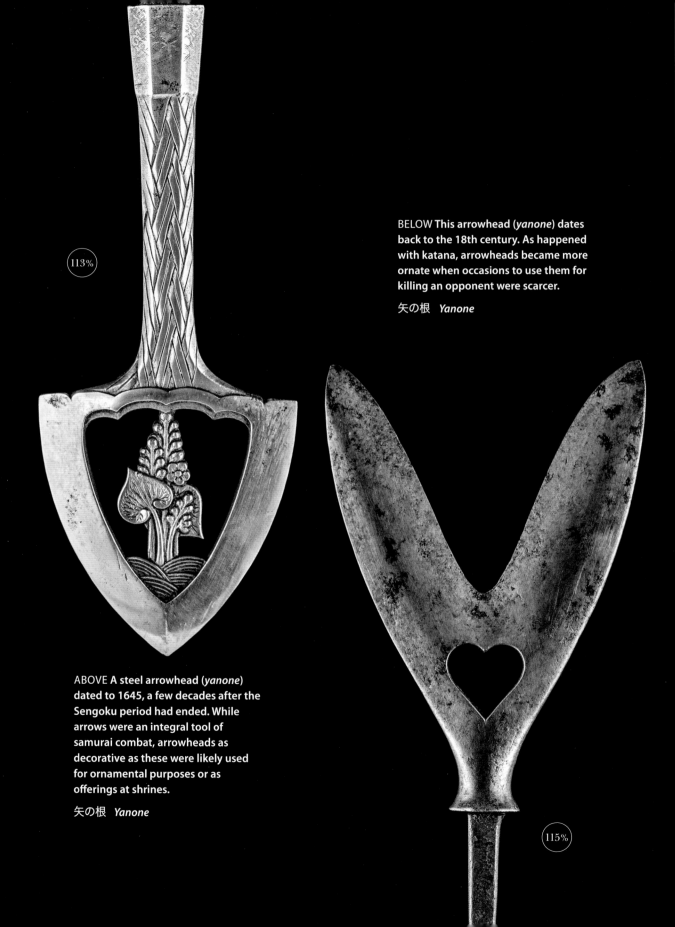

(113%)

BELOW **This arrowhead (*yanone*) dates back to the 18th century. As happened with katana, arrowheads became more ornate when occasions to use them for killing an opponent were scarcer.**

矢の根　*Yanone*

ABOVE **A steel arrowhead (*yanone*) dated to 1645, a few decades after the Sengoku period had ended. While arrows were an integral tool of samurai combat, arrowheads as decorative as these were likely used for ornamental purposes or as offerings at shrines.**

矢の根　*Yanone*

(115%)

ABOVE A print representing actor Ichikawa Danjuro II playing Soga Goro, who is sharpening an arrow. The title of the popular play, a story of revenge set in the 12th century, is *Ya no Ne* (arrowhead).

鳥居 清峰 Torii Kiyomine (1787–1868)

PAGES 60–61 A woodblock print of the last stand of the Kusunoki clan at Shijo-Nawate in February 1348, a major battle during the power struggle between Southern Court of the Ashikaga shogun against the Northern Court of the Emperor Go-Daigo.

歌川 国芳 Utagawa Kuniyoshi (1798–1861)

槍 YARI SPEARS

An array of polearms, or *yari*, also brought death to more people than swords in samurai medieval warfare. Most were double-bladed and designed for stabbing, they ranged from smaller spears designed to be used in confined spaces, to long *nagae yari*, which could stretch to 21¼ feet (6.5 meters). In between, there were crescent-shaped blades, triple-bladed spears, asymmetrical blades and even triangular-shaped blades. By the 16th century, *ashigaru* maneuvering in close formation were the backbone of battlefield armies, sometimes integrated with lines of soldiers bearing firearms. Mounted samurai also used spears, the momentum of a horse's gallop adding to the deadly force of the weapon. Spears, and the earlier *naginata* (glaive), were also used to injure and dismount horseback riders. The *naginata* was essentially a curved sword mounted on a shaft; it was also a popular weapon among warrior monks and became the representative weapon studied by women of samurai families to defend the homestead. *Naginata* is practiced as a martial art in contemporary Japan, primarily by women.

RIGHT **Taira no Tomomori (1152–1185) wearing armor and court robes, carrying a** *naginata,* **from the series** *Mirror of Our Country's Military Excellence* **by Utagawa Kuniyoshi. Tomomori, son of Taira no Kiyomori, jumped overboard from his ship during the defeat by the Minamoto at the Battle of Dan-no-ura, the last stand of the Taira clan.**

歌川 国芳 **Utagawa Kuniyoshi (1798–1861)**

平知盛

清盛の四男宗盛
の兄へ智勇と武の
勝ると兄重盛の功を
顕朝と義仲義兵の時
謀を進めず宗盛愚
なりして用ゐず味方都を
止れども宗盛従はず
其子知明父小少だと一の谷まで義経
替へに羽死を致さん小文治元年義経
捕るとに神器二戦小切勝宗盛父子を生
馬る此時帝へ水へあやまた知盛今
是まで人大碇を身ふりのぎ
郷の名将平家随一の
大傑なり

鉄砲 TEPPO FIREARMS

In the early 1540s, a couple of Portuguese traders were among the passengers on a Chinese ship blown by a typhoon onto the island of Tanegashima, south of Kyushu. Along with being the first Europeans to visit Japan, they also had with them a small number of arquebuses, a musket-like weapon. Early Chinese firearms had made their way to Japan via the Ryukyu Islands (Okinawa) over the previous century, but these European weapons were of better quality, if still wildly inaccurate by modern standards. The samurai lord of Tanegashima was impressed enough by a demonstration of their firepower to spend a great deal of money to buy two of the arquebuses and instruct his best swordsmith to copy them. Legend has it that the swordsmith later traded his daughter to another Portuguese visitor in exchange for further insights into gun making. What is beyond doubt is that the island became so associated with firearms that all across Japan guns came to be referred to as *tanegashima*.

Firearms spread during the Sengoku period and near to the domain of the Satsuma, one of the most bellicose samurai clans in the nation. Within a decade, hundreds of thousands of arquebuses are reported to have been manufactured in Japan. Before the century was out, firearms played a decisive role in the Battle of Nagashino (1575), where Oda Nobunaga's deployment of arquebus units against the mounted samurai of the Takeda clan is often cited as a turning point in Japanese warfare.

RIGHT **An Edo period illustration from a series by the artist Yamaguchi Bisu in 1848 showing an *ashigaru* foot soldier. The soldier is depicted with an arquebus musket and wearing a *jingasa* hat, as well as the two swords traditionally carried by samurai. The inscription reads "later generation ordinary soldier."**

山口 美崇 **Yamaguchi Bisu (19th century)**

後世雑兵

城 SHIRO CASTLES

The simple wooden stockades of the early centuries of the samurai were superseded by larger complex structures utilizing more stone by the Sengoku era. The rise of firearms also impacted castles, leading to stone constructions that could withstand volleys from arquebusiers. Military historians note that this was in contrast to Europe, where the introduction of the cannon brought the demise of castles. By the end of the 16th century, concentric stone walls typically surrounded a *honmaru* main compound and a *tenshukaku* central keep.

Many of the early fortresses were *yamajiro* or mountain castles, situated on rocky slopes like Takeda Castle, built in the first half of the 15th century in what is now Hyogo Prefecture. Takeda Castle was captured by the warlord Toyotomi Hideyoshi in the unification campaigns and was abandoned in the early 17th century. The foundations have been restored and it is now famous for the way it protrudes above clouds of fog on cold mornings.

To the south of Takeda Castle on the western approach to Kyoto is Himeji Castle, a prime example of a *hirayamajiro*, a castle built on a hill surrounded by flat plains. Himeji Castle was rebuilt and expanded from the 14th to 17th centuries and is the largest castle in Japan, consisting of multiple maze-like layers of a moat, gates, fortifications and 83 buildings in a complex covering 233 hectares (576 acres). Also referred to as White Heron Castle for its white exterior that resembles a flying bird, the extremely well-preserved Himeji Castle has survived World

War Two bombing and earthquakes, and was featured in the 1967 James Bond film *You Only Live Twice.*

Another well-preserved fortress is Matsumoto Castle in modern day Nagano Prefecture, a *hirajiro* or plains castle, a type which had become commonplace by the 16th century. Sitting on flat land, such fortresses were usually surrounded by castle towns or *jokamachi*, where merchants and other ordinary folk lived under the protection of daimyo. Matsumoto Castle is known for its main keep and two smaller towers inside three concentric baileys.

Of the hundreds of castles that once dotted feudal Japan, only around a dozen have survived the disparate dangers of battles, compulsory destruction orders by shoguns, fires, earthquakes and disrepair due to neglect over the centuries.

RIGHT **Oda Nobunaga (1534–1582), the first of the three unifiers of Japan, on horseback surrounded by retainers while surveying repairs on his castle. This woodblock print was created in the mid-19th century by Utagawa Kuniyoshi.**

歌川 国芳 **Utagawa Kuniyoshi (1798–1861)**

大多春永

坂井右近

八鳥半蔵

保里蘭丸

田津川左近

塩加波伯耆守

宅間玄蕃

千場田辰家

一魁齋
國芳画

A woodblock print from the Edo period by Utagawa Sadahide (1807–1873)—depicting Kusunoki Masashige's defense of Chihaya Castle for the Emperor Go-Daigo in 1333 against the forces of the Hojo clan. Kusunoki is hailed as an ideal samurai for loyalty to the emperor.

歌川 貞秀 Utagawa Sadahide (1807–1873)

Another print by Utagawa Sadahide of the
Siege of Chihaya. The siege is famous for
the ingenuity of both the attackers, who
used portable bridges to scale the walls,
and the massively outnumbered defenders
under Kusunoki, who employed guerilla
tactics, the castles mountainous setting
and dummy warriors.

歌川 貞秀 Utagawa Sadahide (1807–1873)

Himeji Castle, the finest extant example of a Japanese castle, in a print by Utagawa Sadahide. Himeji was built in the mid-16th century, but had existed in other forms for centuries beforehand. It has appeared in a James Bond film, as well as Akira Kurosawa's *Kagemusha*.

歌川 貞秀 Utagawa Sadahide (1807–1873)

鎧 YOROI ARMOR

As all of the samurai's primary weapons—swords, spears, bows and arquebus—were two-handed, carrying a shield was not practical. Katana were then used as shields to parry other swords or spears, but the samurai predominantly relied on body armor to protect them in combat. The *o-yoroi* armor is, with its distinctive rectangular protective plates for the shoulders and thighs, the most recognizable type worn by the samurai, though it fell out of favor during the Sengoku period as warfare shifted away from horseback archery towards infantry and guns. Consisting of small scales tied together and lacquered leather panels, along with additional plates to protect vital areas, topped off with a metal facemask and *kabuto* helmet, a mounted samurai in full *o-yoroi* would have cut an imposing figure on the battlefield.

Over the centuries, developments in armor included the introduction of iron plates for the shoulders, thighs and torso to protect against arquebus shot, along with tighter-fitting sleeve guards which allowed more fluid movement. It is said that Tokugawa Ieyasu, the shogun who unified Japan, removed his armor after a battle to find several bullets which unbeknown to him had pierced his plating but not the inner layers.

Similar to classic katana, the finest surviving suits of armor are regarded as works of art.

LEFT The *yoroi* style of armor consisting of a *kabuto* helmet, *kusazuri* plates that hung from the *do* breastplate, was distinguished by rectangular shoulder guards and *kusazuri*. After falling out of use in the 14th century, it came back into favor in the Edo period, when it was more ceremonial than practical. This suit is from the 19th century.
鎧 *Yoroi*

RIGHT A well-preserved set of full samurai armor dating from 1662, known as *tosei gusoku* or full modern armor, with a breastplate (*do*) made of iron, gauntlets and sleeves, partly in response to the introduction of firearms to the battlefield. The breastplate is adorned with an image of the fearsome Buddhist deity Fudo Myoo (Acala), who was worshipped as a defender of the nation, and two of his acolytes.
当世具足 *Tosei gusoku*

二枚胴具足

NIMAI-DO GUSOKU
TWO-PIECE CUIRASS ARMOR

Front and back views of a set
of 18th century armor with a
two-piece cuirass (*nimai-do
gusoku*) and *kabuto* helmet
emblazoned with the crest
(*mon*) of the Mori clan. The style
of the armor harks back to the
o-yoroi (great armor) more
popular during the centuries
before the Sengoku era.

二枚胴具足 *Nimai-do gusoku*

面頬 MENPO
FACE GUARD
(FACE MASK)

LEFT This mid-19th century armor features the protective face mask known as *menpo* or *mengu*. Samurai armor evolved over time in response to various innovations in the art of warfare, from the introduction of firearms in the 16th century to the influence of European armor and advances in the use of materials. It could take a year to make a suit of armor.

面頬 *Menpo* or 面具 *mengu*

RIGHT An 18th century suit of *yoroi* armor made out of wood, metal, lacquer, leather, silk and cotton, from the collection of the National Gallery of Victoria in Australia. The bowl-shaped *gusoku*-style helmet shows the influence of European armor that had made its way to Japan by this time. The clan's *mon* (crest) is visible on the *do* breastplate and the *haidate* (thigh guards.)

鎧 *Yoroi*

BELOW An example of an Edo period *kawari kabuto*, literally "strange helmet," which had figures of animals, gods or various other objects mounted on top of them. *Kabuto* were constructed from materials including iron, gold-copper alloy, lacquer, leather, silk, wood, gesso, bone and gesso binder.

変り兜 *Kawari kabuto*

RIGHT This armor of the Matsudaira clan, complete with a face mask (*menpo* or *mengu*), on display at the Musée national des arts asiatiques-Guimet (Guimet National Museum of Asian Arts) in Paris. A full suit of armor like this weighs between 77 and 143 lbs (30 and 65 kg).

面頬 *Menpo* or 面具 *mengu*

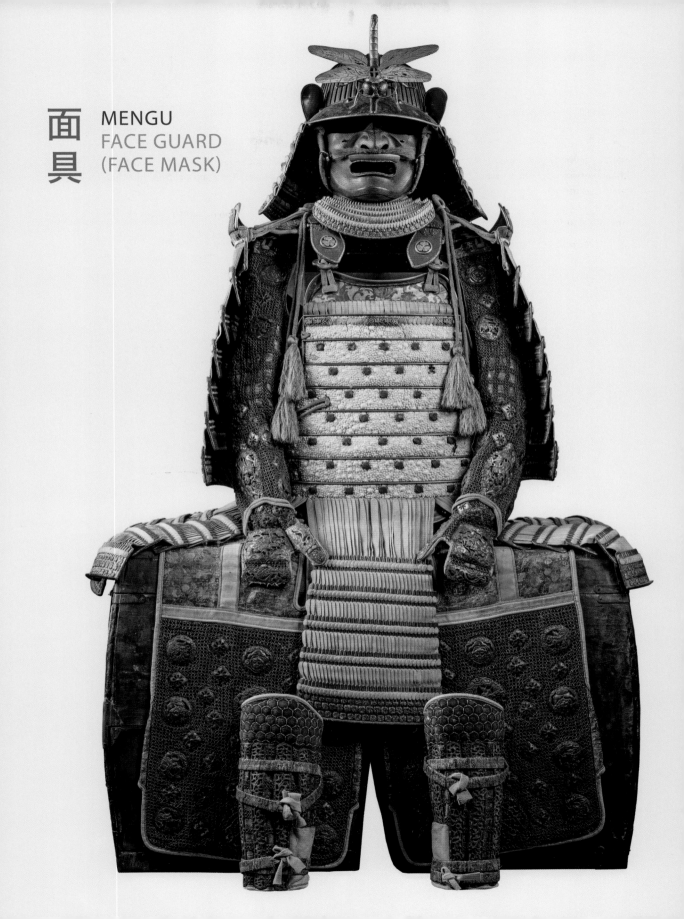

面具

MENGU
FACE GUARD
(FACE MASK)

A *kabuto* helmet from the 15th century with the style of extended crests (*datemono* or *tatemono*) that would fall out of fashion and then be revived in the Edo period. An ornate sun sits between the horns, which are intricately engraved at their base.

立物 *Datemono* or *tatemono*

胴

DO
BREASTPLATE

A set of armor with a breastplate (do) made of steel, russet iron and lacquered leather, along with gold details, made by Unkai Mitsunao in the late 17th century, from the British Museum's collection. Unkai was known for his distinctive *kabuto* helmets.

Unkai Mitsuhisa (雲海光尚, also known as Mitsunao, active 1670–1705 ca.)
胴 *Do*

筋兜
SUJI-KABUTO
RIDGED HELMET

A *suji-kabuto* helmet, made from multiple plates, a type commonly worn by high-ranking samurai in the 15th and 16th centuries, though this helmet dates from the 18th century. The shape, bulbous at the back and sloping down to the front and center, is called *akoda-nari* due to its similarity to the *akodauri*, a squash-like fruit.

筋兜 *Suji-kabuto*

一の谷馬藺兜

ICHINOTANI BARIN KABUTO
ICHINOTANI STYLE HELMET WITH IRIS LEAF DESIGN

This Ichinotani style helmet with iris leaf design dates from the 16th or 17th century: the strikingly protruding crest would leave nobody who saw it in any doubt that the wearer was a samurai of great importance and status.

一の谷馬藺兜 *Ichinotani barin kabuto*

具足
GUSOKU
MODERN ARMOR

Gusoku armor from the 17th century with hinged iron breastplate to allow greater flexibility of movement. Such designs were unusual in the 17th century and most associated with the powerful Uesugi clan and their close allies.

具足 *Gusoku*

角頭巾
SUMI-ZUKIN
SQUARE HAT

A *kabuto* helmet in the style of *sumi-zukin*, a kind of hat worn by priests and doctors. This flamboyant 16th century helmet is topped with a fiery Buddhist deity Fudo Myoo (Acala) on a thin sheet of iron. The lacquered plates at the back would have had a *shikoro* neck guard attached to them.

角頭巾 *Sumi-zukin*

陣羽織 JINBAORI
SURCOAT

RIGHT **A back view of a red *jinbaori* from the 18th or 19th century showing the three-leaved hollyhock crest. *Jinbaori* were sleeveless and designed to be worn over armor, though this was made for a child.**

陣羽織 *Jinbaori*

ABOVE **A late 16th century surcoat (*jinbaori*) made from imported wool from Europe and silk from China, it bears the Naito clan crest on the back. Only three examples of such *jinbaori* from this period are still in existence.**

陣羽織 *Jinbaori*

This particularly colorful and ostentatious *jinbaori* features an intricate design on the inside. Such expensive and luxurious clothing was worn only by the highest-ranking samurai and daimyo.

陣羽織 *Jinbaori*

CHAPTER 5

THE SENGOKU PERIOD:
AN AGE OF CEASELESS WAR

If there was a period in the history of Japan that can be called the age of the samurai, it was the Sengoku period. Named for an era of Chinese history which unfolded more than two thousand years earlier, it can be translated as the Age of the Nation at War or the Warring States period. Though there were major battles preceding and succeeding it, the Sengoku period was a tumultuous era of almost ceaseless conflict which raged for almost a century and a half. The outbreak of the Onin War marked its outset, while its conclusion brought about the true unification of the nation under the Tokugawa shogunate.

The catalyst for the Onin War was again two powerful houses vying for control, but this time over shogunal rather than imperial succession. The heirless Ashikaga Yoshimasa was more interested in immersing himself in the appreciation and practice of cultural arts at his Ginkaku-ji (Silver Pavilion) in Kyoto than being shogun, the authority of which was already in decline. Yoshimasa had convinced his younger brother Yoshimi to leave his life as a monk and succeed him, when a year later in 1465, a male heir was unexpectedly born to the shogun. The Hosokawa clan lined up behind Yoshimi, while the Yamana clan supported the installing of the child Yoshihisa as military ruler.

The dispute erupted into open warfare within the city of Kyoto in 1467, with more than 160,000 troops opposing each other. In the middle of the fighting, in 1473, the heads of both clans perished, Yoshimi switched sides, Yoshimasa stepped down and at the tender age of eight, Yoshihisa succeeded him. Victory

saw the Hosokawa clan in control of an enfeebled shogunate, accelerating nationwide social upheaval and warfare between emboldened daimyo.

TAKEDA SHINGEN 武田 信玄

Eleven years of pitched battles had brought ruination to Kyoto and drew samurai allies into fighting across the land. During World War Two, Kyoto was spared the devastation wrought on most Japanese cities by bombing raids, and so today when its citizens talk of a building or temple being "destroyed in the war," it is the Onin War they are referring to.

RIGHT Takeda Shingen (1521–1573), a daimyo famous for his military prowess and rivalry with Uesugi Kenshin for control of the Kanto region of eastern Japan during the late Sengoku period. His nickname was "The Tiger of Kai," for the province he hailed from (now Yamanashi prefecture, southwest of Tokyo.)

歌川 国芳 Utagawa Kuniyoshi (1798–1861)

The instability of the period during and after the Onin War facilitated uprisings in the provinces, which in turn weakened the power of the shogun and his allies. At the heart of these were the Ikko-ikki, alliances of peasant farmers, Buddhist warrior-monks, Shinto priests and low-ranking samurai, which rebelled against daimyo and the shogun. The most notable of these was in 1487–8 in Kaga province. An Ikko-ikki of more than 100,000 soldiers defeated the forces of the local daimyo Togashi Masachika, after he had returned from fighting for the shogun Ashikaga Yoshihisa to put down the uprising. Masachika committed seppuku in his besieged castle, leaving the common folk in charge of the domain for nearly 100 years.

The rebellions of the Ikko-ikki were representative of the phenomenon of *gekokujo*—the low overcoming the high—during the Sengoku period, which also saw storied clans annihilated, an impotent imperial court and shogunate, as well as minor samurai overthrowing established daimyo.

Against this chaotic background, rival daimyo fought each other as alliances continually shifted and betrayal abounded. In 1493, deputy shogun Hosokawa Masamoto led a coup d'état which replaced one Ashikaga shogun with another and effectively removed any vestige of central government authority. So disrupting was this coup that some historians now cite it as the start of the Sengoku period. By the turn of the century the Hosokawa clan was wrought with internal strife and would be at war with itself within decades.

UESUGI KENSHIN 上杉 謙信

One of the great rivalries of the time was between Takeda Shingen and Uesugi Kenshin, whose Battles of Kawanakajima, fought on the same river plain in Nagano every year from 1553 to 1557, and again in 1563, became the stuff of samurai legend. Two skilled tacticians, with respected generals under them, they commanded tens of thousands of well-disciplined and equipped soldiers.

Two incidents from their warfare stand out in particular.

Shingen's military campaigns were funded with the gold that had for centuries been mined in his mountainous Kai province, but he was left short of another less glamorous commodity during one of his extended battles with Kenshin. The Hojo clan cut off supplies of salt to Shingen's forces, something Kenshin thought unsporting when he got wind of it. Kenshin had salt from his own province delivered to his rival, reportedly accompanied by a message stating: "I fight not with salt, but with a sword."

On another occasion the two warlords were said to have come to direct blows in a brief but famous clash during the fourth Kawanakajima battle, the bloodiest of the series. The Uesugi forces attacked in waves and were breaking through the Takeda lines, when Kenshin himself made it all the way through to the curtained command tent or *baku* (such tents were the source of the bakufu name for shogunate governments). Unable to reach his sword, Shingen had to fight Kenshin using an iron *tessen* war fan, more commonly used for signalling, until one of his retainers speared his rival's horse and ended the duel.

RIGHT **Uesugi Kenshin (1530–1578), known as "The Dragon of Echigo" (the Echigo domain is in today's Niigata prefecture) for his martial skills, and for his battles with Takeda Shingen. Both of the warlords took Buddhist vows, though this in no way tempered their taste for violence or lust for power. This print** Lord Uesugi Terutora Kenshin and His Retainers, **from the series** Mirror of Famous Generals with Their Four Leading Retainers (Meisho Shiten Kagami)**, shows Kenshin with some of his vassals, senior samurai who served him.**

歌川 芳虎 Utagawa Yoshitora (active ca. 1836–1887)

PAGES 92–93 **Scene from one of the Battles of Kawanakajima** (Kawanakajima no Kassen) **between Takeda Shingen and Uesugi Kenshin, probably the fourth engagement in 1561, when the two warlords reportedly came to direct blows in an incident which only added to their legend. The depiction of mounted archery and closer combat with katana and** naginata **reflects the reality of most large-scale samurai conflicts of the era.**

歌川 芳員 Utagawa Yoshikazu (active ca. 1848–1870)

名将四天鑑　上杉輝虎謙信公

本庄越前守繁長

柿崎和泉守景家

甘粕近江守景時

直江山城守兼続

上金板

ABOVE Another depiction of the Kawanakajima battles, also probably the fourth, showing the Takeda and Uesugi armies fighting along the banks of the Chikuma River, near modern-day Nagano. The print is titled *Shinshu Kawanakajima Ogassen*, meaning "The great battle at Kawanakajima in Shinshu," which may refer to a nearby temple where records of the battle were found.

歌川 芳虎 Utagawa Yoshitora (active ca. 1836–1887)

YAMAMOTO KANSUKE 山本 勘助

RIGHT **Yamamoto Kansuke (1501–1561), one of the "Twenty-Four Generals of Takeda Shingen."** A military strategist known for his victorious pincer movement tactics at the fourth battle of Kawanakajima. Tragically for him, the samurai mistakenly thought his plan was failing and charged into the enemy ranks, perishing alongside his two senior retainers.

歌川 国芳 Utagawa Kuniyoshi (1798–1861)

大日本六十余将

尾張

織田上總介

信長

春亭

京鶴記

信長ハ桓武天皇の後胤
平相國清盛の嫡男小松内府
重盛の二男新三位資盛の男
親眞寿永の乱み父資盛
西海子没する時未幼子あり
其母是を抱ふ江州津田の
郷（流落す時ハ越前
織田の荘の神職此幼子を
養ひ家を續んと織田權大夫親眞とし
其子孫相續して後尾州ふ移る親眞十七代の
孫備後守信秀の男上総介信長十四才ゆて
三州吉良大濱ふ發向し後永禄三年今川
義元を掃狭間ふ討取り尾張一國を領す亦美濃の
齋藤竜興を遂て美濃の國を領し岐阜の城ふ
移る其猛威強大なり斯て義昭公の頼ふ依て
補佐して逆賊三好松永を平ぐ然れども義昭公愚ふして自滅なり
遂ふ信長左近衞大将を兼天下の政を司る高運英傑の将ふり

ODA NOBUNAGA 織田 信長

Meanwhile, a warlord by the name of Oda Nobunaga was rising to prominence in the lands around modern day Nagoya. At the 1560 Battle of Okehazama, using familiarity with local terrain and a surprise attack after a storm, Nobunaga routed the 25,000-strong army of Imagawa Yoshimoto with a force around a tenth its size, cementing his reputation as a shrewd general. Nobunaga went on to form a temporary alliance with Takeda Shingen and a longer lasting relationship with Tokugawa Ieyasu as he began to consolidate power. By 1568, he was able to install Ashikaga Yoshiaki as the 15th shogun of his line, though real authority now largely rested with Nobunaga.

After defeating other rival daimyo, Nobunaga turned his attention to the Ikko-ikki, who though they resisted samurai rule were not averse to allying with them if it served their ends. In the early 1570s Nobunaga's forces destroyed Ikko-ikki strongholds at

Nagashima and butchered thousands of warrior monks and commoners, including women and children, at the Enryaku-ji fortified complex of

OPPOSITE **Oda Nobunaga (1534–1582) holding a** *naginata* **by Utagawa Yoshitora, another artist of the Utagawa school of ukiyo-e. Nobunaga was a wild and eccentric youth but went on to become one of the unifying warlords of the Sengoku era; he was an ally and later sworn enemy of Takeda Shingen.**

歌川 芳虎 **Utagawa Yoshitora (active ca. 1836–1887)**

BELOW **The** *Battle at Okehazama* **by Ikkaisai (Tsukioka) Yoshitoshi, last of the great ukiyo-e masters. The battle was a decisive victory for a much smaller force under Oda Nobunaga over the Imagawa clan, bolstering Nobunaga's reputation and status as an eminent warlord.**

一魁斎 (月岡) 芳年 **Ikkaisai (Tsukioka) Yoshitoshi (1839–1892)**

monasteries overlooking Kyoto. In 1576, he laid siege to Ishiyama Hongan-ji, the huge temple fortress of the Ikko-ikki on the site of what is now Osaka Castle. Considered impregnable, it took 11 years to capture, the longest siege in the nation's military history.

Nobunaga was fighting on multiple fronts, against former ally Takeda Shingen, Uesugi Kenshin and the forces of the shogun he had installed. He did though have the support of Tokugawa Ieyasu, who defeated the Shingen's army after an initial setback in 1573. One of the most decisive battles of the era saw Nobunaga and Ieyasu meet the Takeda and its allies at Nagashino in 1575. Nobunaga's deployment of staggered volley-fire from lines of arquebusiers protected by stockades and spearmen devastated the Takeda cavalry and is credited with changing Japanese warfare.

Having unified much of the country, Nobunaga was betrayed by one of his top generals Akechi Mitsuhide in 1582 while visiting Honno-ji temple in Kyoto for a tea ceremony. Nobunaga committed seppuku as his assailants closed in and his eldest son Nobutada was killed in the fighting. Revenge was exacted by Toyotomi Hideyoshi, another supposedly loyal lieutenant, who some suspect was in on the plot, but certainly became a beneficiary of it. Hideyoshi, who was born to peasant stock with no family name and rose through the ranks of Nobunaga's regime, waged war against Akechi's allies and any members of the Oda clan who refused to bow down to him.

The Battle of Nagashino (1575) saw the Oda and Tokugawa clans defeat the Takeda in a bloody engagement that took the lives of 18,000 of the 53,000 combatants, mostly from the defeated Takeda. The painting focuses on the lines of Nobunaga's riflemen, many of them *ashigaru* soldiers drawn from the ranks of the peasant class, who decimated the Takeda cavalry charges using volley fire, making the battle a turning point in the use of firearms in Sengoku warfare.

長篠の戦い **Nagashino no Tatakai**

Betrayed by one of his generals, Akechi Mitsuhide, for reasons unclear, Oda Nobunaga committed seppuku rather than be captured by the soldiers of his treacherous attacker at Honno-ji temple in Kyoto, where he was preparing for a tea ceremony. Nobunaga reportedly ordered the temple set ablaze so that his head could not be taken, though this is not depicted in this ukiyo-e print.

楊斎延一 Nobukazu Yosai (1872–1944)

The *Siege of Busanjin fortress*, a silk painting by Korean artist Byeon Bak (1742–?), showing samurai attacking the Korean port in 1592, the first stage in a planned invasion of Ming China ordered by Toyotomi Hideyoshi. The arquebus matchlock guns of the Japanese were a pivotal factor in the initial victory though the Japanese would eventually withdraw from the Peninsula.

釜山鎮の戦い *Busanjin no Tatakai*

THE JAPANESE INVASIONS OF KOREA AND THE BATTLE OF SEKIGAHARA

The 1590 siege of Odawara Castle, about 43½ miles (70 km) southwest of Tokyo, where 220,000 troops loyal to Hideyoshi eventually overcame the 80,000 defenders, broke the Hojo clan and eliminated one of the last obstacles to his power. Some regard the battle as the end of the Sengoku era, but fighting was not yet at an end.

Hideyoshi had already issued edicts outlawing European Christian missionaries, who had converted large numbers of both samurai and commoners, and went on to conduct a census and severely restrict the movement of people within the country. The *katana-gari* edict confiscated swords from the entire population except samurai and their retainers on the pretext of using the metal for a giant statue of the Buddha. This move conveniently disarmed any potential uprisings.

Absolute power appeared to have gone to Hideyoshi's head and he soon settled on a foolhardy plan to invade Ming China. Opting to execute this scheme via an invasion of the kingdom of Korea, two campaigns on the Peninsula in the 1590s followed similar patterns. 150,000-strong samurai armies made initial gains, only to be hampered by supply problems, guerrilla warfare by Korean defenders and reinforcements from China, leading to eventual withdrawal in 1598. The expeditionary force was actually ordered to return by the Council of Five Elders, a panel of daimyo established by Hideyoshi

before his death in September 1598.

In true Sengoku fashion, divisions arose on the council after Hideyoshi's passing, with Tokugawa Ieyasu leading the faction advocating military over civilian rule. The conflicts came to a head in 1600 at the Battle of Sekigahara, where nearly 200,000 troops faced off; Ieyasu's forces and the clans of Eastern Japan against the clans loyal to Hideyoshi's infant son, mostly from the west. The betrayal and shifting alliances commonplace during the era were taken to extreme levels at Sekigahara, when a number of daimyo secretly courted by Ieyasu with promises of land and titles actually switched sides mid-battle.

Victory for Ieyasu was decisive and he stripped the many of the daimyo who had opposed him of their domains and distributed them among his supporters. He was appointed shogun by the Emperor Go-Yozei in 1603, aged 60, launching the Tokugawa shogunate which would rule Japan for 250 years. He officially ruled for just two years, abdicating in favor of his son Hidetada, but in reality wielded power without being tied up with ceremonial duties. There was one last major battle to be fought to eliminate Toyotomi Hideyori, son of Hideyoshi, who some disaffected daimyo were aligning with. The siege of Osaka Castle wiped out what was left of the Toyotomi clan, and with it, any challenges to the authority of Ieyasu and the Tokugawa shogunate. The nation was no longer at war.

Chinese and Korean forces assault the
Japanese-built castle at Ulsan in 1598. The
smaller force of samurai, under daimyo Kato
Kiyomasa, held the fortress and eventually
routed the attackers despite suffering heavy
casualties. Rivalry with campaign commander
Ishida Mitsunari led to his success at the Siege
of Ulsan being played down in reports. Kato
would take his revenge on Ishida by fighting
against him during the Sekigahara campaign.

蔚山城の戦い Urusan-jo no Tatakai

ABOVE *The Battle of Sekigahara* in October 1600, where Tokugawa Ieyasu, supported by numerous daimyo mostly from eastern Japan including Kato Kiyomasa and Date Masamune, defeated disgruntled clans loyal to the Toyotomi. It was one of the largest and most important battles of the Sengoku era, leading to the establishment of the Tokugawa shogunate, the long-lasting but final government of samurai.

関ヶ原の戦い *Sekigahara no Tatakai*

PAGES 108–109 *The Siege of Osaka Castle*, the stronghold of the Toyotomi clan, lasted from 1614 to 1615 and ended with a victory that handed total control of Japan to the Tokugawa shogunate. This screen painting depicts the summer siege of 1615, where more than 150,000 Tokugawa warriors eventually took the castle. The battle was followed by centuries of relative peace.

大坂夏の陣 *Osaka natsu no jin*

CHAPTER 6

LEGENDARY SAMURAI
FROM MUSASHI TO YOSHITSUNE

Widely regarded as one of the greatest swordsman to have wielded a blade, Miyamoto Musashi in some ways embodied the ideal of a samurai, and yet was most atypical in others. Born in the 1580s, his father a retainer of the local daimyo and skilled swordsman, Musashi studied the martial ways from a young age and claimed to have killed a samurai in single combat at aged 13. There are stories of him fighting at both the Battle of Sekigahara and the Siege of Osaka Castle, with some accounts placing him on different sides of the conflicts. What seems surer is that he took a *musha shugyo* warrior pilgrimage around Japan in the early 1600s, taking on the best swordsmen he could find. He went undefeated in more than 60 duels, many against the finest exponents of their art, and often employing wooden swords against katana or other deadly weapons.

MIYAMOTO MUSASHI 宮本 武蔵

His most famous duel was against master swordsman Sasaki Kojiro on a tiny island between Honshu and Kyushu in 1612. Legend has it that Musashi arrived three hours late, likely to unsettle his opponent, and stepped from a boat carrying only a wooden sword he had fashioned from an oar (presumably a spare) during the journey. His angry opponent attacked first, only to be countered by a fatal rib-breaking and lung-puncturing blow from Musashi. Having proved himself the best in the land, Musashi foreswore deadly duels, though continued to test himself as he journeyed across the nation.

Musashi's travels took him from Edo (Tokyo) to Osaka, though for reasons unclear, his offers to become a sword teacher to various lords were rebuffed. He finally settled as a guest of the Hosokawa of Kumamoto Castle in Kyushu in 1640, receiving a

samurai stipend, teaching his two-sword Niten Ichi-ryu to local warriors, and engaging in art, poetry and Zen meditation. In the years before his death in 1645, he lived in a cave near Kumamoto, where he wrote *The Book of Five Rings* (*Gorin-no-Sho*), a book on strategy and life that has been studied by martial artists and businesspeople worldwide. For a man who had little significance in history, Musashi has had an outsized impact through his ideas and the numerous portrayals of him in popular culture.

RIGHT Legendary swordsman Miyamoto Musashi portrayed by Nakamura Utaemon IV, a member of a lineage of kabuki actors which remains active to this day. This ukiyo-e print by Utagawa Kunisada was produced during the 1830s.

歌川 国貞 Utagawa Kunisada (1786–1865)

LEFT A portrayal of Miyamoto Musashi in a print by Utagawa Kuniyoshi from the series *The Sixty-Nine Post Stations of the Kisokaido Road*. Musashi can be seen preparing to attack a giant bat from what appears to be some form of cable car.

歌川 国芳 Utagawa Kuniyoshi (1798–1861)

RIGHT Another portrait of Miyamoto Musashi by Utagawa Kuniyoshi, this one from the series *Eight Hundred Heroes of the Japanese Shuihuzhuan*, believed to date from around 1830. Here Musashi can be seen battling a tailed monster. Numerous tales surround Musashi, and distinguishing truth from legend is no simple task.

歌川 国芳 Utagawa Kuniyoshi (1798–1861)

PAGES 114–115 Miyamoto Musashi's famous duel against Sasaki Kojiro in 1612, depicted in an Utagawa Yoshitora ukiyo-e. Accounts vary as to what happened during the encounter, one of the few certainties being that Sasaki died. The title is *Miyamoto Musashi Fights Sasaki Ganryu at Ganryujima in Kyushu*. The island was originally called Funajima. Kojiro's real name was Ganryu, not Sasaki as he is usually known today.

歌川 芳虎 Utagawa Yoshitora (active ca. 1836–1887)

KUSUNOKI MASASHIGE 楠木 正成

Born in 1294 of unclear lineage, Kusunoki Masashige would many centuries later be held up as a paragon of samurai loyalty. What made his loyalty noteworthy was, somewhat strangely, that it was to the emperor and not a daimyo or shogun. When the Emperor Go-Daigo went to war in 1331 against the Kamakura shogunate, which had ruled since the Minamoto had defeated the Taira more than a century previously, Kusunoki answered the call.

After an attack by shogunate forces on the imperial "rebels," Kusunoki found himself holed up at the wooden fortress of Akasaka, near what is today Osaka, massively outnumbered. Defending a fortress with little fortification, Kusunoki kept his attackers at bay with a combination of disciplined archers, cunning tactics and ingenious improvisation. The bakufu army found themselves under barrages of rocks, boiling water and huge logs released from the slopes of the hill on which the fort stood, as well as a wall attached to the real fortification which collapsed on the assailants. Having pulled back from an assault on the walls, they found themselves under attack from a force which Kusunoki had positioned in reserve on another hill nearby. In the chaos, Kusunoki himself led a charge from the fortress into the startled shogunate samurai, driving them into a long retreat. As supplies ran low, the wily general had a funeral pyre built of the bodies of the fallen. He and his troops escaped in small groups at night through the forested hills, leaving one samurai to light the flame. When the attackers arrived at the fort, they were convinced by the story of the single weeping defender mourning the mass suicide of his comrades-in-arms.

Kusunoki's defense of the nearby mountaintop castle of Chihaya two years later was a military masterclass against a force 50 times the size of his 2,000-strong garrison. In addition to his previous tactics, he employed armored dummies to lure attackers into vulnerable positions and a brilliant double-cross that led to the shogunate forces attacking their own. The siege held until an imperial army relieved Kusunoki and his men.

Ashikaga Takauji had been a general of the bakufu at the two sieges, but switched sides to support the emperor. After the imperial forces were victorious he expected to be appointed to a senior position, perhaps even shogun. Angry that this reward was not forthcoming, Takauji turned again and marched on Kyoto with a large army.

Kusunoki recommended retreating to Mt. Hiei, enlisting the help of the warrior-monks of Enryaku-ji—site of the infamous massacre by Oda Nobunaga's forces two centuries later—and waging guerilla warfare on Takauji's troops once they settled in Kyoto. Apparently reluctant to leave the capital, the emperor insisted Kusunoki ride out to meet the coming shogunate army on the field.

Despite knowing this meant almost certain death, Kusunoki obeyed his Emperor and his army was duly decimated at the Battle of Minato River in 1336. Kusunoki and his brother, along with their retainers, committed suicide, declaring they wished for seven lives to give to the emperor. This display of loyalty saw Kusunoki's memory resurrected in the 19th century by the samurai behind the Meiji Restoration, and again by the Imperial Army in World War Two. A statue of Kusunoki stands to this day outside the Imperial Palace in Tokyo.

RIGHT **Minamoto no Tametomo's (源 為朝) prowess as an archer was said to stem from his drawing arm being much longer than the other. He is on a beach holding a bow in this print, by Ikkaisai (Tsukioka) Yoshitoshi, in which he is referred to as Chinzei Hachiro, another name he was known by.**

一魁斎 (月岡) 芳年 **Ikkaisai (Tsukioka) Yoshitoshi (1839–1892)**

Kusunoki Masashige Chihayajo rojo no zu (*Kusunoki Masashige on the Road to Chihaya Castle*) by Utagawa Yoshifuji from the mid-19th century, shows the warrior, famed for embodying the ideal of loyalty, preparing for his celebrated defence of Chihaya Castle. The castle was designed by Kusunoki and leveraged the natural defences offered by the 3,691-feet (1,125-meter) Mount Kongo on which it stood.

歌川 芳藤 Utagawa Yoshifuji (1828–1887)

MINAMOTO NO YOSHITSUNE 源 義経

A truly tragic samurai hero, Minamoto no Yoshitsune's life has been extensively portrayed in Japanese literature, theater and books. Exiled to a monastery in Kyoto as a child after the death of his father, he was later sheltered by the Fujiwara lord Hidehira in the northeast. Little is known of his younger years and many of the stories surrounding him, such as his defeat of an infamous bandit boss at just 15, are likely apocryphal. According to another, he seduced the daughter of a daimyo so that he could read the lord's copy of Sun Tzu's seminal strategy book *The Art of War*.

What seems beyond doubt is that his tactical genius and bravery in famous victories for the Minamoto over the Taira clan earned him not just honor and briefly-held titles, but the suspicion of his half-brother Yoritomo, who was wary of his sibling's success.

Betrayed by Yoritomo, then head of the Minamoto and soon to be first of the Kamakura shogun, and finding his lands confiscated, Yoshitsune decided to head to the safety of the northeast with a small band of his trusted men disguised as Buddhist monks. It is during this journey that one of the most celebrated tales of Yoshitsune is said to have occurred. At a checkpoint manned by Yoritomo's men at Ataka, in Ishikawa Prefecture on the Sea of Japan coast, his loyal retainer, the giant Benkei, played the part of the senior monk and strikes Yoshitsune for some alleged clumsy behavior. The guards are supposedly convinced that nobody would dare beat a samurai lord and therefore the victim cannot be Yoshitsune. Other versions of the story, which has been told in numerous forms, have the guards recognizing the fugitive, but letting him pass out of respect for Benkei's loyalty.

Back in the lands of his childhood protector Hidehira, Yoshitsune had a few short years of peace until soon after the lord died in 1187. Hidehira's son turned on Yoshitsune, in an attempt to win favor with Yoritomo, leading 500 men in an assault on the mansion where the exiled Minamoto was staying. Here another legend was born. The warrior-monk Benkei is said to have stood guard on the narrow bridge to the residence and dispatched no fewer than 300 attackers. Terrified to engage him in further close-quarter combat, Benkei was riddled with arrows, but still stood tall. When the Fujiwara soldiers eventually dared to approach the unmoving monk, they found he was literally dead on his feet. His trusty retainer's actions bought Yoshitsune the time to perform seppuku.

Even in death, the myth of Yoshitsune lived on. Accounts from the Ainu people of the north reported that he escaped and made his way to Hokkaido. Another legend has it that when the shogun Yoritomo was killed in a riding accident in 1199, it was the ghost of Yoshitsune that startled his horse. An even more fantastical theory, which appeared centuries later, is that Yoshitsune carried on from Hokkaido to the Asian mainland and re-emerged as none other than Genghis Khan.

Utagawa Yoshitora's *The Night Attack of Kumasaka at Akasaka Station* in Mino province depicts a 15-year-old Minamoto no Yoshitsune (then known as Ushiwakamaru) fighting an infamous bandit Kumasaka Chohan and his cohorts. Yoshitsune became a celebrated general of the Minamoto, but was eventually hunted down by warriors sent by his half-brother Yoritomo, who would go on to be shogun.

歌川 芳虎 **Utagawa Yoshitora (active ca. 1836–1887)**

Gojo Bridge, an Episode from the Life of Yoshitsune shows the young Minamoto samurai on the bridge where he defeated the giant warrior monk Benkei. After their duel, the two became trusted companions until their death, when Benkei is said to have held off a large unit of attackers for long enough to give his lord time to permit seppuku and experience an honorable demise.

大蘇 (月岡) 芳年 Taiso (Tsukioka) Yoshitoshi (1839–1892)

CHAPTER 7

FEMALE SAMURAI

The age of the samurai was undoubtedly a male-dominated world. Nevertheless, there were women on the battlefields and their stories are often overlooked. Recent studies and DNA testing on bodies excavated from sites of Sengoku era battles have found as many of 30% of them were women. What proportion of them were actually combatants is difficult to ascertain, but there is no doubt that more women were involved in fighting than is widely believed. Both women of samurai families who were trained to fight to defend their families and those who rode out to battle alongside men were known as *onna-bugeisha* or *onna-musha* (female martial artists). The standard weapon of these women was the *naginata*, a slightly curved blade mounted atop a polearm. The *naginata* is practiced as a martial art in modern Japan and its disciples are predominately female. A *kaiken* dagger was also carried by female samurai, to be used in self-defense or for suicide if they were in danger of being captured.

TOMOE GOZEN 巴 御前

One of the most celebrated female warriors was Tomoe Gozen, variously described as wife, mistress or concubine of the warlord Minamoto no Yoshinaka, who fought alongside him in the Genpei War. Tomoe is reported to have killed seven samurai at the Battle of Yokotagawara in 1181 and decapitated one of Minamoto no Yoritomo's finest warriors at the Battle of Awazu in 1184. According to the *Heike Monogatari* (*The Tale of the Heike*), the epic poem about the conflict: "She was also a remarkably strong archer, and as a swordswoman she was a warrior worth a thousand, ready to confront a demon or a god, mounted or on foot."

After the second battle of Uji River, she is dismissed by the retreating Yoshinaka, apparently concerned about his image if he died alongside a woman. She gallops into a group of 30 mounted opponents, dispatching a few of them before riding off into the sunset, never to be heard of again. Other accounts have her captured and forced to become a concubine, or a nun, and living until the age of 91.

Tomoe Gozen (1157–1247), probably the most renowned female warrior of the samurai age—though historical records of her life are very limited—from a series of ukiyo-e prints *Mirror of Beauties Past and Present* by Ikkaisai (Tsukioka) Yoshitoshi. Some historians doubt whether Tomoe actually existed, believing her to likely be an amalgamation of female warriors of the time.

一魁斎 (月岡) 芳年 Ikkaisai (Tsukioka) Yoshitoshi (1839–1892)

鞆繪女

信州木曽の住人中原兼任が女にて源義仲の妾なりし
容色艷麗なして勇力偉丈夫に超たり
義仲兵を北國に舉に及び兄兼平と倶に軍陣ぞ
從事し義仲の為に一方の將として勳功例
四天王稱根平の上出づ壽永二年の戰ふ宇治の
手駒ふ破遂ず義仲出死の覺悟ろて軍勢
と押出て自巳に今日を限りぞ其日の
直垂に緋威の冑を縫しろ
出立花弓に秋の千草を縫へしる
態と脱捨て白布たゝんで

鉾卷ー
春風と名づくる信濃牧の
荒駒ふ金泥を以て三巴の摺箔を
ある金鞍あして打跨り黑漆に
金の蛭卷ーたる太刀を水車の如くおふふて
先登ふ進んで勇戰ー五隊の陣を打やぶり
坂東の勇士數多打取る
勅使河原兄第内田三郎を始め坂東の勇士數多打取る
遺言ふより戰場を切拔信濃ふ隱る後鐮倉ふ召れ和田義盛の
有様より味方ふわりおつて
あるが如敵り離て
感ぜぬ者ふりしとぞ斯て義仲の

画工 月岡米次郎
山板大倉孫兵衞梓

Tomoe Gozen and Wada Yoshimori (1147–1213) as portrayed by actors, in a ukiyo-e by Utagawa Kuniyoshi. In one of the many legends around Tomoe Gozen, after she was captured by Wada Yoshimori, a commander for Minamoto no Yoritomo's army, she was forced to be his concubine. In another, she became a nun.

歌川 国芳 Utagawa Kuniyoshi (1798–1861)

Tomoe Gozen Killing Uchida Saburo Ieyoshi at the Battle of Awazu no Hara by Ishikawa Toyonobu shows Tomoe defeating one of the famous warriors she is said to have overcome during the last stand of Minamoto no Yoshinaka in 1184.

石川 豊信 Ishikawa Toyonobu (1711–1785)

HANGAKU GOZEN 板額 御前

An uprising in the early years of the Kamakura shogunate which followed the Genpei War saw another woman stake her place in samurai history with her battlefield exploits. Hangaku Gozen (Gozen was a term akin to lady) of the Taira clan, like Tomoe, said to have been both beautiful and deadly. She was a leader in the defense of a fort against a much larger force. A skilled archer and wielder of the *naginata* from horseback, her prowess allegedly had many of the opposing samurai begging for her hand in marriage after she was injured. But the shogun Minamoto no Yoriie apparently heard of her beauty and exploits, and had her brought to the capital at Kamakura, where he forced her to marry one of his senior retainers.

OHORI TSURUHIME 大祝 鶴姫

During the Sengoku period, a teenage female fighter by the name of Ohori Tsuruhime made a name for herself after becoming head priestess of a shrine on the island of Shikoku when her father and older brothers were killed. Trained in the arts of war since childhood, she led an army against invading samurai from the mainland, personally killing the opposing general on his flagship during a naval battle. Fighting against the same samurai clan two years later, she committed suicide, aged 17, when her lover was killed in the battle.

IKEDA SEN 池田 せん

A few decades later, another female warrior, Ikeda Sen led a unit of 200 riflewomen at two important battles during the 1580s, fighting alongside the forces of the Tokugawa, Toyotomi and Oda clans.

Hangaku Gozen would have been a contemporary of Tomoe Gozen who fought in the Genpei War. She is shown here in full mounted samurai armor in this ukiyo-e print *Yoshitoshi's Incomparable Warriors: Woman Han Gaku* from the late 19th century.

大蘇 (月岡) 芳年 **Taiso (Tsukioka) Yoshitoshi (1839–1892)**

武田勝頼の夫人
夫人ハ北条氏康の女ふして
後に勝頼に嫁す天正年間勝
頼織田信長の為に敗北して
天目山ふ逃る夫人之を送
よ゛ふ勝頼死せんとわつ
て夫人をさとして脱まめん
とを夫人泣て曰く伉麗の情
豈ふ変る可けんやさるゝ
ちカゞを取つて夫と共に自
殺せりと云ふ

LADY HOJO 北条 夫人

LEFT Lady Hojo (1564–1582), the second wife of Takeda Katsuyori, son of Takeda Shingen. Katsuyori was defeated at the Battle of Tenmokuzan by the forces of Tokugawa Ieyasu and Oda Nobunaga. He pleaded with his wife to flee, but she refused and committed suicide alongside him and their children.

安達 吟光 Adachi Ginko (active 1874–1897)

TAMAYORI-HIME 玉依 姫尊

ABOVE Tamayori-hime, wife of Taira no Atsumori, shown at the seashore carrying a *naginata*. Atsumori was killed aged 17 by Kumagai no Jiro Naozane in a famous incident at the Battle of Ichi-no-tani in 1184. Tamayori-hime was carrying his unborn child and is said to have traveled far and wide searching for her husband after hearing rumors he was still alive.

歌川 国芳 Utagawa Kuniyoshi (1798–1861)

WOMAN KANSUKE かんすけ

BELOW **This print by Ikkaisai (Tsukioka) Yoshitoshi** *The Woman Kansuke Slaying an Assailant with a Sword* **dated November 1886, shows what is likely a man dressed as a woman, but may be a woman, despatching an enemy with a katana. The inscription states, somewhat cryptically, "Woman Kansuke fooling many of his enemies by looking feminine."**

一魁斎 (月岡) 芳年 Ikkaisai (Tsukioka) Yoshitoshi (1839–1892)

LADY YATSUSHIRO 八代

RIGHT **A woodblock print depicting the legend of Lady Yatsushiro, who is said to have gone into battle while pregnant, fending off arrows with a** *naginata* **and accompanied by her fighting wolf Nokaze. The print by Utagawa Kuniyoshi dates from the mid-19th century.**

歌川 国芳 Utagawa Kuniyoshi (1798–1861)

PAGES 134–135 **These two prints are part of a triptych entitled** *Chiyoda Castle* (*Album of Women*) **by Yoshu (Hashimoto) Chikanobu showing female samurai carrying** *naginata*. **In a late 19th century ukiyo-e, Chiyoda Castle, built in 1457, was also known as Edo Castle, and became the seat of power of the Tokugawa shogunate in the early 17th century. It now sits within the grounds of the Imperial Palace in Tokyo. In 1701, it was the site of the incident which led to the events of the famous tale of the** *47 Ronin*.

揚州 (橋本) 周延 Yoshu (Hashimoto) Chikanobu (1838–1912)

ONNA-BUGEISHA 女武芸者

Photographs of *onna-bugeisha* (or *onna-musha*), female warrior samurai. While the *naginata* was the predominant weapon for women of samurai families, some did practice the way of the sword, particularly during the Edo period. There is evidence for female samurai having participated in some of the major battles during the Sengoku era and fighting to defend their families on many occasions.

NAKANO TAKEKO 中野 竹子

LEFT AND RIGHT Images of Nakano Takeko (1847–1868), an *onna-bugeisha* of the Aizu domain and acknowledged as a highly proficient exponent of the martial arts. She is said to have been inspired by tales of the female warrior Tomoe Gozen during her childhood. She fought in a female unit at the Battle of Aizu during the Boshin War, where she died wielding a *naginata*.

MYTH AND REALITY

Separating the wheat of fact and reality from the chaff of fantasy and mythology in history is never an easy task. This is more challenging when dealing with a group as romanticized, and even fetishized, as the samurai. The ideal samurai was unquestionably loyal, unflinchingly brave, indefatigably chivalrous and tirelessly in pursuit of perfection in every aspect of his life. But, being flawed humans, it was not unusual for samurai to fall far short of such ideals.

There are also misconceptions about the *bushi* which have resulted from inaccurate portrayals in popular culture. A prime example is the way samurai are associated with the katana, when for much of their early history they were primarily mounted archers. Indeed, it was during the Tokugawa shogunate (1603–1868) that the katana came to define the samurai, for they were the only people allowed to carry them; yet this was a period when their blades were rarely drawn in anger, if at all, and the samurai functioned mostly as leaders, administrators or even accountants.

A significant misunderstanding with regards to samurai is that they lived their lives according to a standardized canon of beliefs called Bushido, literally "the way of the warrior." Although many samurai houses did have rules, they varied considerably depending on locality and the era. The rules more often than not represented the ideal and certainly not the reality of their existence.

One of the most famous books associated with a ubiquitous romantic ideal of the *bushi* is the *Hagakure* (*Hidden by the Leaves*), written in the early 18th century but largely forgotten until a new edition was published in 1900. Based on the musings of Yamamoto Tsunetomo, an administrative retainer of a Kyushu lord, his pen was certainly mightier than his sword. Japan had been at peace for a century and Yamamoto's writings bear the mark of an old man's grumblings about the shortcomings of the younger generation and a pining for a world where samurai could maintain a sense of urgency to their calling in spite of the peaceful era they lived in. The book gained a new lease of life during Japan's imperialistic expansion in Asia in the first half of the 20th century, and was utilized as propaganda to show the troops the samurai ideals they should aspire to.

Perhaps even more curious is *Bushido: The Soul of Japan*, published in 1899. It was written in English by Nitobe Inazo, who had received his higher education in English before traveling to America then Europe to further his studies. Nevertheless, his book came to be seen by many as an insight into the true nature of the Japanese, even by some Japanese themselves, once it had been translated into his native language in 1908. In any case, it is important to remember that there was no such thing as a one-size-fits-all codified Bushido during the Sengoku era, but the samurai did cultivate idiosyncratic norms and ideals peculiar to their calling as professional warriors and the politics of era in which they lived.

None of this is to say that the samurai were not a remarkable collection of individuals worthy of attention, study, admiration or even emulation in some aspects. Deeds of awe-inspiring loyalty were not unknown, but neither were acts of shameless betrayal. Let us not forget Ashikaga Takauji, who switched allegiances twice during the Genpei War, before ordering the execution of many of his kin while establishing his shogunate. Or the samurai lords who helped change Japanese history by changing sides in the middle of the Battle of Sekigahara. For every tale of a retainer who followed his lord in death by committing seppuku in a practice known as *junshi*, there is one of a samurai who turned on his daimyo, clan or even brother because it was expedient to do so.

Ritual suicide by excruciatingly painful self-disembowelment certainly points to a psyche of a warrior class that separates it from many of its counterparts elsewhere. Seppuku or the less formal hara-kiri—the two words are written with the same characters but reversed—was performed with a *tanto* dagger or *wakizashi* (short sword). The records of the earliest seppuku are from the late 12th century with two senior Minamoto samurai the most likely candidates for having first died in this fashion.

Seppuku came in many forms and could be performed for disparate reasons. Defeat in battle, imminent capture, bringing disgrace upon their lord, clan or name, were all grounds for suicide. Later, the practice developed of daimyo or shogun ordering samurai to commit seppuku as a judicial punishment, though the real reasons were sometimes far less than judicious.

If time and circumstances permitted, seppuku involved an elaborate ceremony. The samurai would write a death poem, don a white kimono known as a *shini-shozoku*, drink a cup of purified sake and take a hold of his blade with cloth. Plunging the weapon into the left side of the abdomen, he would tear it

Reizei Takatoyo, referred to as Reizei Hangan Takatoyo in this print by Ikkaisai (Tsukioka) Yoshitoshi, committing hara-kiri in 1551. Legend has it that after cutting open his abdomen, he threw his guts at the ceiling. This woodblock print is from a series known as *One Hundred Warriors*.

一魁斎 (月岡) 芳年 **Ikkaisai (Tsukioka) Yoshitoshi (1839–1892)**

across to his right side, in preparation for further cuts. It was at this point, and often before, that the *kaishaku* second would finish the job through decapitation. The *kaishaku* could be a retainer, friend, comrade or even victorious adversary honoring his defeated foe. Many *kaishaku* stepped in early to spare agony, executing a *daki-kubi*, which ideally left the head attached to the body via a sliver of flesh. It was not unknown for *kaishaku* who botched their task to in turn commit seppuku in atonement.

Women of samurai families also took their own lives on occasion, usually by cutting the neck arteries with a dagger, sometimes following their husbands or

to escape the abuse which commonly followed capture. Before a female samurai committed suicide, she would commonly bind her legs together over her kimono to prevent her falling into an undignified posture as she died. Such concern with honor after death was the case with the wife of Onodera Junai, one of the 47 Ronin, whose suicide was depicted in an ukiyo-e woodblock print.

The story of the *47 Ronin* is one that has had a legion of retellings in Japanese popular culture, as well as a Hollywood movie version in 2013. A dispute between a young daimyo Asano Naganori and a senior official of the Tokugawa shogunate Kira Yoshinaka resulted in the former cutting the latter with his short sword inside Edo Castle, a capital offence. Asano was stripped of his domain and ordered to commit seppuku. His retainers became master-less samurai, or ronin, who bided their time and plotted their revenge. Two years later, in 1702, they converged on Kira's residence in the capital, and after fighting their way past the lord's guards, cut off his head after he failed to apologize for dishonoring their late daimyo. The ordinary folk of Edo were by all accounts very taken with their upholding of samurai values and celebrated as they laid Kira's head on the grave of their fallen leader at Sengaku-ji Temple. The shogunate ordered they commit seppuku, rather than execute them as common criminals, cementing their status as samurai heroes. Not everyone was equally impressed. The curmudgeonly Yamato is recorded in the *Hagakure* as stating that true samurai would have taken their revenge immediately, and they should

Obata Sukerokuro Nobuyo was a young retainer whose lord went missing at the Battle of Sekigahara. After being captured, Sukerokuro was brought before Tokugawa Ieyasu himself, who, impressed at the young samurai's refusal to tell of his lord's whereabouts, released him. Sukerokuro went straight to Omi-ji Temple and committed seppuku.

一魁斎 (月岡) 芳年 **Ikkaisai (Tsukioka) Yoshitoshi (1839–1892)**

have at the very least committed seppuku immediately after their mission was accomplished at Sengaku-ji, where they were eventually buried.

The *Hagakure* also had stern advice on an often-overlooked facet of samurai culture: A young man should test an older man for at least five years, and if he is assured of that person's intentions, then he too should request the relationship. A fickle person will not enter deeply into a relationship and later will abandon his lover.

It was common for samurai to take a young steward to mentor in the martial ways, etiquette and values of the *bushi*, and also for them to become lovers. These relationships were supposedly consensual and exclusive, though did not preclude them from taking female partners, and generally continued until the young warrior came of age. The practice was, like so much of samurai culture, codified into a system, which became known as *wakashudo*, the way of adolescent boys.

Though the relationships were regarded as ennobling for both parties, there are multiple accounts of disputes and revenge killings sparked by the jealousy of male lovers. There are euphemistic references to "beloved retainers" of senior samurai in the literature and historical records of the time, as well as love letters between *bushi*. Those recognized as having engaged in *wakashudo* include Minamoto no Yoritomo, the first shogun; most of the Ashikaga shoguns, including Takauji, who is said to have formed a cavalry corps of his young lovers known as the *hana-ikki* or flower unit; the three warlords who unified Japan; Uesugi Kenshin; and Miyamoto Musashi.

The practice continued into the Edo period, when it became commonplace among wealthier urbanites, and only came to be seen as taboo after the Meiji Restoration and the subsequent influence of Christian-influenced morality from the West.

If there is a warrior culture that has been more mythologized than the samurai, it is perhaps that of the ninja, with the two sometimes erroneously portrayed as sworn enemies. Reliable records of their activities are scarce and the term "ninja" didn't even

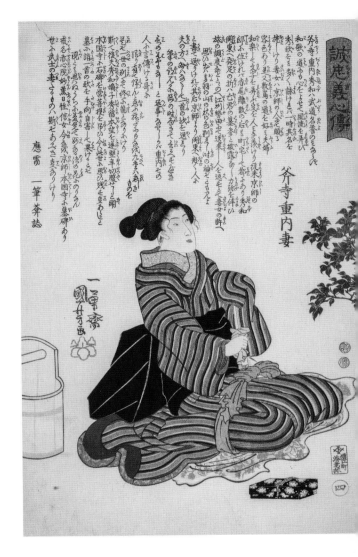

The wife of Onodera Junai, one of the 47 Ronin, preparing to commit suicide using a knife hidden in her sleeve in this ukiyo-e print by Utagawa Kuniyoshi. Note her legs are tied together to stop her falling into an un-ladylike position after her death

歌川 国芳 Utagawa Kuniyoshi (1798–1861)

The Harakiri of Oishi Kuranosuke Yoshio shows the leader of the 47 Ronin, Oishi Yoshio, preparing to commit seppuku, with a *kaishaku* second ready to cut his head off. The entire group were ordered to perform ritual suicide by the Tokugawa shogunate, only adding to their legend and reputation. The fact that they were allowed to commit seppuku rather than being executed was likely in part due to the high regard of the ordinary citizens of Edo, who saw them as heroes for their actions.

近藤 樵仙 Kondo Shosen (ca. 1866–1951)

岡島八十右衛藤原常樹

勘定頭

禄二十五石

原元辰のおとうと
岡島氏を嗣ぐ
性強氣ふして鎗劍
ふ達さ主家凶變の後浪花ゝ
住ゝ腰痛を病で有馬の温泉
ふ至る途中山賊五七人ふらぞ
あひるにことぐくらっぜ並木の松ふ
そゝ付けむきしとぞ其勇此一更を以て志ビ

法号
双袖拂劍信士 行年四十才

OKAJIMA YASOEMON TSUNESHIGE
岡嶋八十右衛門常樹

LEFT Okajima Yasoemon Tsuneshige, one of the 47 Ronin, carrying what appears to be the head of Kira Yoshinaka, who they killed in revenge for the death of their lord, Asano Naganori. This print by Ikkaisai (Tsukioka) Yoshitoshi was part of a series *Pictorial Biographies of the Loyal Retainers*.

一魁斎 (月岡) 芳年 Ikkaisai (Tsukioka) Yoshitoshi (1839–1892)

OISHI YOSHIO 大石 良雄

ABOVE Oishi Yoshio carrying a *naginata* spear. In this print, from a series called *Portraits of Loyal and Righteous Samurai*, he is titled as Oboshi Yuranosuke Yoshio, the name given to his character in the many plays about the 47 Ronin, known as *Chushingura*.

歌川 国芳 Utagawa Kuniyoshi (1798–1861)

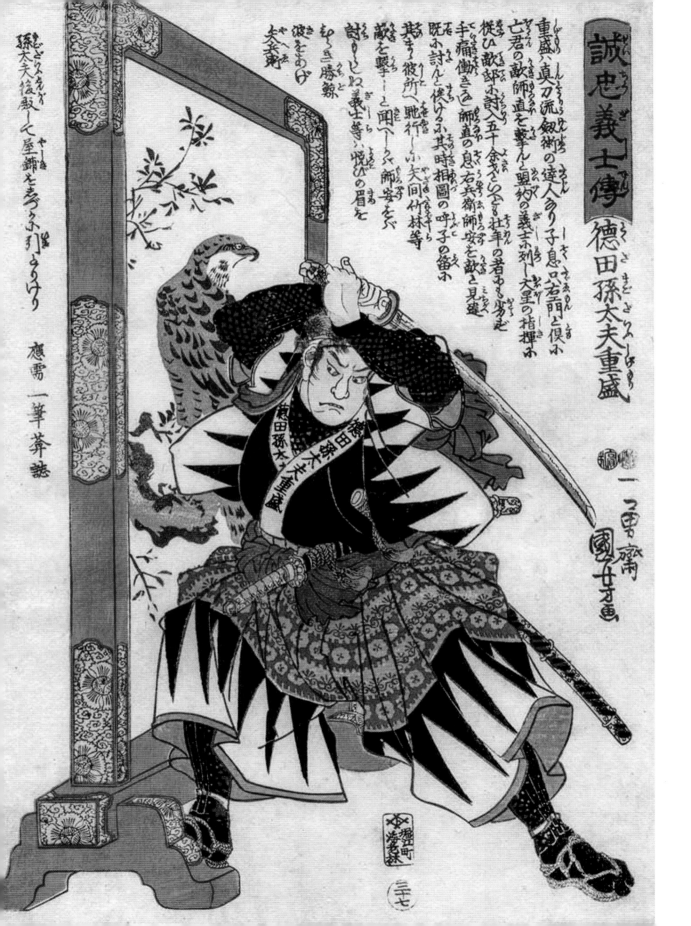

LEFT **Okuda Magodayu Shigemori, a renowned swordsman, during the revenge attack of the 47 Ronin. His son Sadaemon (also known as Yukitaka) joined his 50-year-old father in the killing of Kira Yoshinaka. From the** *Biographies of Loyal and Righteous Samurai* **series.**

歌川 国芳 **Utagawa Kuniyoshi (1798–1861)**

come into use until the 20th century. There is evidence of groups of men skilled in espionage, subterfuge, assassination and guerilla warfare hailing from the village of Koka (Koga) and the province of Iga, in a mountainous region southeast of Kyoto. Indeed, those proficient in such ways were often referred to as *Iga no mono* (guy from Iga), or *shinobi*, from the word stealth.

During the Sengoku period, units of *shinobi* were hired by samurai clans to engage in intelligence gathering, assist in siege-breaking, and missions of murder. However, some of those who worked as *shinobi* were also samurai, there was no clear differentiation.

Surviving scrolls suggest they employed a variety of techniques, devices and weapons, including explosives, traps, poisons and blades. The quintessential image of a black-clad figure stealing across a rooftop on his way to single-handedly dispatch a band of samurai retainers using *shuriken* throwing stars, murder their lord and then disappear in a puff of smoke is, disappointingly enough, largely a creation of 20th century pop culture.

ABOVE **Detail from an Utagawa Kuniyoshi print representing** *Chushingura* **(***47 Ronin***) of the attack on the Edo (Tokyo) residence of Kira Yoshinaka, a Tokugawa shogunate official whose actions led to their lord committing seppuku. The samurai retainers waited nearly two years to exact their revenge and the story has become one of the most famous in Japanese history and popular culture.**

歌川 国芳 **Utagawa Kuniyoshi (1798–1861)**

PAGES 148–149 **These two prints are part of a triptych by Utagawa Kuniyoshi titled** *The Night Attack in the Storehouse of Loyal Retainers* **(***Chushingura youchi no zu***) showing the assault on Kira Yoshinaka's house. The tale of loyal samurai revenge has been told in numerous plays, books and films over the years.**

歌川 国芳 **Utagawa Kuniyoshi (1798–1861)**

CHAPTER 9

BUSHI IN PEACETIME:
SAMURAI, ZEN AND THE ARTS

The teachings of Zen Buddhism, an offshoot of the Chan tradition from China, first arrived in Japan in the seventh century, but failed to gain traction in its new home until many hundreds of years later. The rise of the samurai followed a somewhat parallel trajectory, and by the time they were consolidating power in the 13th century, Zen was beginning to spread among them and other elites.

Two monks, Eisai, who also introduced the drinking of tea from China, and Dogen, were instrumental in disseminating Zen philosophy in the early 1200s. The attraction to the samurai of Zen teachings such as the ephemerality of life, self-discipline and a unity of thought and action is easy to imagine. There were a large number of prominent samurai who embraced Zen, including Hojo Tokimune, the shogun at the time of the attempted Mongol invasions. Indeed, Tokimune consulted his Zen master Mugaku Sogen, a monk from Song China, for advice at the time of the crisis, who perhaps predictably told him to meditate. Tokimune is credited with spreading Zen and exiled the monk Nichiren, head of an eponymous rival Buddhist school, to Sado Island.

Legendary swordsman Miyamoto Musashi's *The Book of Five Rings* seems to bear the hallmarks of Zen influence, not least of which is some extremely esoteric, vague and occasionally contradictory pronouncements. But the notion that Musashi was a dedicated student of Zen was propagated in stories centuries after his death. Similarly, the narrative that most *bushi* were somehow the living embodiment of Zen is one that became widespread much later, primarily after their demise. Like the tales of samurai and Bushido, much of the belief in a Zen-infused warrior class stems from books in the Meiji period and the 20th century, and has been challenged by more recent scholarship, which points to a more nuanced picture of the relationship between the two.

While many *bushi* did genuinely embrace elements of Zen practice and tenets, it was far from universal. Some found Zen teachings esoteric and impenetrable, and there were samurai houses which championed its temples for reasons of political or economic expedience. There were also numerous samurai followers of rival Buddhist doctrines: Tendai, Shingon and Jodo (Pure Land). Still others, particularly in Kyushu, converted to Christianity and adopted Christian names. Some samurai continued to practice Christianity secretly after the sometimes brutal persecution of believers in the 16th and 17th centuries, as evidenced by *tsuba* katana hand guards later discovered with images of crosses and crucifixes hidden inside them. Mostly, however, samurai were

A painting from a hanging scroll of samurai indulging in pleasures of the flesh, likely a scene from an upscale brothel. The picture, by an unknown artist, is titled *Yuraku-zu*, literally a "picture of amusement" and dates from around 1625. After the Siege of Osaka Castle in 1615, the samurai enjoyed centuries of a largely peaceful existence, and many of those who could afford to enjoyed lives of relative carefree luxury.

遊楽図 *Yuraku-zu*

followers of several religious traditions at the same time, rather than just one or the other.

SAMURAI AND ART

As the *bushi* evolved over time from being warriors from the regions upon whom many in the imperial court looked down their noses on as uncouth ruffians, to wielders of power over that court and the land, their habits and interests also changed. Much of what was regarded as refined culture at the time originated in China, and had followed the same routes as, and was strongly influenced by, Zen: calligraphy, painting, poetry, rock gardens and the tea ceremony (chanoyu or *chado*.)

A well-rounded samurai was expected to be literate and appreciative of art and aesthetics, though

some maintained that the only arts which should be focused on were the martial ones. Ashikaga Yoshimasa, the shogun who had the Silver Pavilion (Ginkaku-ji) built in Kyoto, was held in low regard for his excessive interest in the arts and corresponding lack of interest in the tedious business of actually ruling. Yoshimasa is also credited with helping to formalize the tea ceremony and spread its popularity. Toyotomi Hideyoshi and Oda Nobunaga, two of the feared warlords who largely unified the country, were also known as enthusiastic adherents in the way of tea. Weapons were forbidden in teahouses and one idea was that *bushi* could use the ceremony to clear their minds in the troubled times of the Sengoku period, though Nobunaga is reported to have planned at least one assassination while partaking.

Works of calligraphy and ink paintings by respected samurai also survive, including some by Musashi, along with death poems written before committing seppuku. There are as well accounts of *bushi* even composing verse and engaging in other cultural pursuits during lulls in battles.

Many shogun, daimyo and other prominent samurai were also often great patrons of art and culture, of which there was a somewhat surprising blossoming during the conflict-wrought centuries. As perpetual war gave way to the relative peace of the Edo period in the early 17th century, the ruling samurai class was free to devote more of their time, energy and wealth to artistic endeavors.

PEACETIME WARRIORS

With the nation finally unified under the Tokugawa shogunate at the dawn of the 17th century, and trade and other interactions with the rest of the world all but forbidden, the Edo period witnessed explosive growth in prosperity and distinctly Japanese arts and culture. Though estimates vary widely, the population had likely reached 30 million by 1700, and by the middle of the century, Edo was one of the largest cities in the world, inhabited by more than a million residents.

Tokugawa Japan was organized into a strict hierarchy that was close to a caste system. At the apex was the Imperial court nobility, the shogun and daimyo. Below that came the samurai, accounting for an estimated 5% of the population. The farmers made up another 80%, and the remainder were artisans and merchants. These three occupations were of equal

status, but the merchants were generally the wealthiest of them all, much to the chagrin of the samurai who traditionally held disdain for matters of commerce. Merchant families were known to engage in social climbing via marriage into samurai houses, many of which had become relatively impoverished, forbidden as they were from engaging in business and sometimes severely lacking in financial nous.

There was another caste that existed below this social system, an underclass of untouchables known as *eta* or *burakumin*, literally hamlet people. They were engaged in professions such as sanitation, as well as those connected with death including abattoir workers, undertakers and even leather tanners. These professions were regarded as taboo by both Buddhists and Shintoists. Although the designation was abolished in 1871, discrimination continued well into the 20th century, leading their descendants to be hugely overrepresented amongst the ranks of the yakuza.

The upper echelons of Edo society lived a life that where much of their energy could be focused on the pursuit of art and pleasure. With demonstrations of prowess in battle now impossible, honor and status came with patronage and practice of high culture. Whether it was Noh theater, calligraphy or poetry, art became ingrained in everyday life. Even the tools of war, from elaborate helmets to intricate sword guards, became works of art evaluated on their appearance rather than martial effectiveness.

With the coming of the Meiji Restoration in 1868, led by lower ranking samurai from various domains and some ambitious members of the tiny nobility, Japan began on the path of a rapid drive to modernize and in many ways imitate the West. The new government dissolved the samurai class and forbade them from carrying swords. The era of the samurai was drawing to a swift close. But there would be a last dramatic and tragic samurai hurrah.

THE LAST SAMURAI

The last great *onna-bugeisha* fought in one of the final samurai conflicts, the Battle of Aizu during the

Boshin War that led to the Meiji Restoration in 1868. Nakano Takeko was both a scholastic and martial protégé, working as a *naginata* instructor while still a young woman. She led a female *naginata* unit in the battle against a vast government force and is said to have killed half a dozen warriors before being shot in the chest. Unwilling to have her head taken as a trophy—standard samurai practice—she had her sister, who served alongside her, decapitate her and bury her head under a tree at the local temple.

There were a number of uprisings by disgruntled former samurai, the last and largest of these was the Satsuma Rebellion in 1877, led by Saigo Takamori, who had been an original member of the Meiji government. Like many of the new government, Saigo hailed from the Satsuma domain in Kyushu, but had become disillusioned with the new regime. After resigning, he founded more than 100 military academies in Satsuma, which understandably concerned the government in Tokyo.

Tension turned to hostilities and Saigo eventually raised an army of students from his academies, who were joined by rebellious former samurai, eventually totalling 25,000. The government forces tasked with quelling the rebellion would number nine times that many and they were better supplied and equipped with more modern weaponry, including warships. The Hollywood movie *The Last Samurai* is very loosely based on the events of the rebellion.

After a failed siege of Kumamoto Castle by Saigo, the bloody Battle of Tabaruzaka claimed the lives of thousands and severely weakened the rebels. After further fighting, Saigo's last stand would come at the Battle of Shiroyama in September, 1877. His force of 500 samurai were heavily outnumbered and bombarded by both Imperial artillery and canons from the government fleet in Kagoshima harbor. Saigo was struck by a bullet and accounts vary as to whether he died from his wounds or committed seppuku.

The man many Japanese regard as the last true samurai was dead. Saigo was posthumously pardoned by the Meiji Emperor and has since been hailed as a principled patriotic hero.

This print is the central part of a triptych belonging to the series *Kagoshima senki* (*Chronicles of the War against Kagoshima*) by Chikanobu, which illustrates the fighting that took place during the Satsuma Rebellion of 1877, unleashed under the leadership of Saigo Takamori by former samurai disillusioned with the Meiji government: this woodcut dates back to the same year of the revolt. The film *The Last Samurai* is very loosely based on these events.

揚州 (橋本) 周延 Yoshu (Hashimoto) Chikanobu (1838–1912)

ABOVE *The Suicide of Saigo Takamori* (*Saigo Takamori sepukku no zu*) by Taiso (Tsukioka) Yoshitoshi recreates one of the stories of the death of Saigo Takamori (1828–1877). His forces were defeated at the Battle of Shiroyama, and he is believed to have been either stabbed or shot in the leg, and may have committed seppuku, perhaps on a boat.

大蘇 (月岡) 芳年 Taiso (Tsukioka) Yoshitoshi (1839–1892)

西郷吉之助隆盛

村田新八郎

桐野利秋

西郷隆盛切腹圖

PAGES 156–157 A photograph of samurai of the Satsuma, some of whom would later rebel against the government they fought to establish. The Boshin War, fought from 1868 to 1869, saw young samurai determined to modernize Japan defeat the Tokugawa shogunate and restore the Emperor Meiji, though in a largely symbolic role. Note the mixture of traditional samurai attire and more modern military dress in the picture by Anglo-Italian photographer Felice Beato.

戊辰戦争中の薩摩藩の藩士 Boshinsenso-chu no Satsuma-han no hanshi

394.

ABOVE A photograph of a samurai by Austrian photographer Baron Franz von Stillfried-Rathenitz, who had a studio in Yokohama. The picture, which was colored by hand, is dated 1881, a few years after the samurai had been abolished as a class.

侍の肖像 Samurai no shozo

RIGHT A man modelling as a samurai displays his tattoo, which appears to have been heavily influenced by the style ukiyo-e woodblock prints. Such tattoos would later be adopted by yakuza gangsters. The photograph is believed to date from 1890.

入れ墨のある日本の武士 Irezumi no aru Nihon no bushi

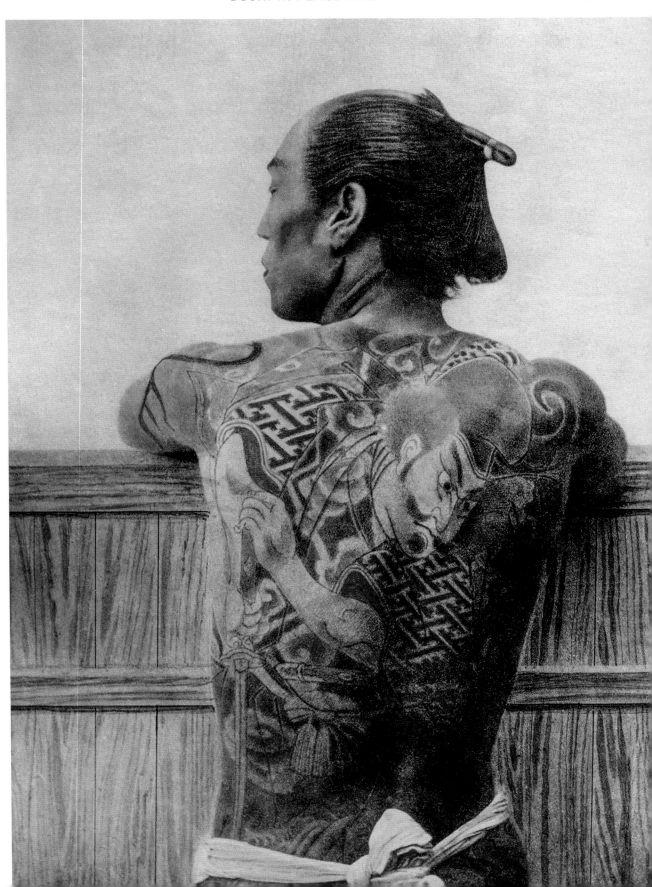

LEFT A samurai in armor photographed by Baron Raimund von Stillfried–Rathenitz (Franz's brother) or his student Kusakabe Kimbei sometime in the 1870s to 1890s. Von Stillfried-Rathenitz owned one of the earliest photographic studios in Japan and trained a number of local photographers.

日下部 金兵衛 Kusakabe Kimbei (1841–1934)

ABOVE A samurai pictured with his helmet, longbows and arrows in 1867, the final year of the Tokugawa shogunate, as the rule of the warrior class over Japan was coming to an end. Photograph by Felice Beato, one of the first Europeans to take pictures in Asia.

ABOVE **Adults and children in samurai costumes at a pageant in a photo believed to have been taken around 1930. The image and ideals of samurai were revived for propaganda purposes during this period as militarism and imperialism took hold. The samurai had cease to exist as a class more than half a century previously, but their influence was still being felt as Japan put itself on a path to a devastatingly self-destructive war.**

LEFT *Daimyo in Armaments* by Austrian photographer and painter Wilhelm J. Burger (1844–1920), who shot in Japan in the early years of the Meiji Restoration around 1869 and 1870. The style of armor harks back to that of before the Sengoku period.

CHAPTER 10

INFLUENCE ON TODAY'S MARTIAL ARTS

Most countries in the world have at least one form of martial arts, but no other nation has produced as many famous codified fighting systems as Japan. The budo of Japan naturally have deep links to its martial history and therefore to the *bushi*. However, the direct influence of the samurai varies considerably between martial arts.

The attraction for some of being a modern day samurai or ninja is clear, and there are those who play on and to such desires, some would say fantasies. This is not to suggest that there is not much to be learned from samurai ideals and methods that can be applied to the study and practice of martial arts. But there exist practitioners and sensei of the more modern budo styles who claim a lineage from the samurai which is tenuous and mistaken at best, or dishonest at worst. In general, the older *koryu* schools, which include armed, unarmed and comprehensive systems, derived their curricula and practice more directly from the battlefield techniques of the samurai; many of the newer styles were in turn influenced by them.

A shift that took place, largely in the 20th century, from more technique and practical focused "*jutsu*" styles to "*do*" arts which place more emphasis on form and character development is also worth considering in the context of samurai influence. An example is how *kyujutsu* samurai archery became the martial art of *kyudo*. The distinction is though far from definitive: *jutsu* can translate as technique, way or art, and *do* as path, way or teachings. It certainly can't be assumed that judo is less effective than jujitsu (*jiu-jitsu*), from which it derived, just because of its *do* suffix.

Somewhat paradoxically, not a few practitioners of the *do*-focused arts regard themselves as guardians of traditional martial values, though their typical emphasis on aesthetics over practicality would stand them in poorer stead in actual combat than those who place a greater emphasis on realistic training.

This is not to say that samurai studied martial arts purely for the purpose of enhancing their battlefield prowess. During the peace of the Edo period, sword schools proliferated and the notion of training the spirit as well as the body became more emphasized, an approach that has significantly impacted modern martial arts.

WAYS OF THE SWORD

The numerous schools of sword fighting practiced by the samurai for centuries, using both wooden (*bokken* or *bokuto*) and live blades, are collectively referred to as *kenjutsu*. Their popularity nose-dived with the demise of the samurai, though practice was continued among the military and police and enjoyed something of a renaissance in the 20th century. *Iaijutsu* or *battojutsu* is a martial art based around the concept of quickly drawing a katana and cutting an opponent, or in practice an object (often rolled up tatami mats.) From this developed *iaido* in the 1930s, though the differences between the two are somewhat blurred.

Some of these styles, or *dojo* (place of the way) within them, practice some form of sparring using *bokken*, usually combined with body armor, but a full-power blow from a solid wooden sword can still cause very serious injury. Due to this, practice with bamboo *shinai*—which began in the Edo period—developed into kendo, the way of the sword, allowing for full speed and power strikes, with practitioners protected by chest plates, padded gloves and face guards.

It is probably safe to say that the various sword arts are more closely linked than others to Japan's legendary warriors, though as previously discussed, the katana was not the dominant weapon for most of their martial history.

KYUDO

Modern day *kyudo* comes in a number of forms, with some schools or *kyudojo* placing more stock in competition versus those that remain dedicated to its practice as a method of active meditation and self-improvement. The 6.5-feet (2-meter) bow is largely unchanged from that once used in feudal Japan, though one notable difference from the days of the samurai is the relatively large numbers of female *kyudoka* (archers). *Kyudo* has gained limited popularity outside Japan, though there is a world cup and other international tournaments.

JUJITSU AND ITS DESCENDANTS

The term jujitsu covers such a plethora of *ryu* (styles), arts and variants—and went on to directly influence so many more—that succinctly describing them all is not possible. At the core of jujitsu are grappling techniques, including throws, sweeps, joint locks and chokes, but some styles also contain strikes and the use of certain weapons. Many of these systems were designed to teach samurai how to fight when they had lost or damaged their primary weapons in battle.

One of the oldest known styles is *Daito-ryu Aiki-jujitsu*, said by some to have been founded by the samurai Minamoto no Yoshimitsu around 900 years ago. Ueshiba Morihei studied *Daito-ryu*, among other jujitsu styles, in the early 20th century, using elements of it to create aikido.

An accomplished educator and later member of the International Olympic Committee called Kano Jigoro also practiced multiple jujitsu styles, which he blended to form judo. Kano was also the originator of the white *gi* training suits and belted grading system since adopted by numerous other martial arts. One of Kano's students Mitsuyo Maeda took the style with him when he emigrated to Brazil. At that point it was still commonly referred to as Kano jujitsu, leading the new art which grew out of it and focused on and refined its ground fighting techniques to be named Brazilian jiu-jitsu.

KARATE

Explanations of movements from karate kata referencing the samurai can be heard in Japanese dojo, while sensei in the West have been known to tell their students that certain moves from the forms were hidden in order to stop them being learned by rival clans during feudal times. The problem with such teachings is that there is simply no evidence that any samurai ever practiced karate.

Karate (meaning empty-hand), originated in Okinawa and was a mix of indigenous styles and systems imported from China, with which the then island kingdom (Ryukyu) had close cultural and trade ties. Indeed, the original characters for karate meant China-hand, but were changed when it was brought to mainland Japan in the early 20th century to play down its foreign lineage.

One of the origin myths of karate is that it was developed by Okinawan peasants to be able to defeat the armored samurai of the Satsuma domain who invaded the kingdom at the beginning of the 17th century and banned the locals from carrying weapons. In reality, the ban applied to firearms and most islanders had been forbidden from wearing weaponry

a century earlier by a local king as part of his measures to abolish feudalism.

Samurai jujitsu did directly influence at least one style of Japanese karate. Shindo Yoshin-ryu was founded by a Kuroda clan retainer in the late in the Edo period and was itself derived from multiple *koryu* schools. The founder of Wado-ryu karate, Otsuka Hironori, studied Shindo Yoshin-ryu and incorporated elements of the joint locks, throws and body shifting he learned into the style he created in the 1930s.

NINJUTSU

As discussed in the Myth and Reality chapter, the historical facts around ninja are open to question and interpretation. Similar things can be said of the modern schools of ninjutsu which claim to teach the skills of the storied operatives from feudal Japan. Some martial researchers and critics maintain that the curricula of the prominent contemporary ninjutsu styles contains little that cannot be found in *koryu* schools such as jujitsu, *kenjutsu* and *bojutsu* (staff/stick fighting). This does mean that their

千代田之御表 武術上覧

techniques are likely to have been drawn from the fighting systems of the samurai, though practitioners point to the study of espionage, subterfuge and psychological methods as differentiating them. Other criticisms levelled at modern ninjutsu include the lack of verifiable evidence of their historical lineage/ authenticity and the absence of pressure testing of techniques through sparring or competition. Most ninjutsu styles use the belt grading system and *gi* that originated from judo, though their training wear is usually black.

The Shogun Views a Demonstration of Martial Arts (*Bujutsu joran*) **presents a scene of a display of kendo at Edo Castle (Tokyo) before the watchful eye of the military leader of the feudal government. This late 19th-century print is part of the series** *Chiyoda Castle (Album of Men)*; **Chiyoda Castle is another name for Edo Castle.**

揚州 (橋本) 周延 **Yoshu (Hashimoto) Chikanobu (1838–1912)**

A TRUE SAMURAI ART

One example of a martial art with a genuine samurai lineage is Tenshin Shoden Katori Shinto-ryu. Founded in the 15th century, it is a truly comprehensive system which teaches a number of sword arts, use of spears, *naginata*, staffs and *shuriken* darts, as well as hand-to-hand jujitsu. Practitioners can even study tactical deployment of troops, the use of fortifications and ninjutsu. A number of notable samurai swordsmen practiced the style, some of whom went on to found their own schools.

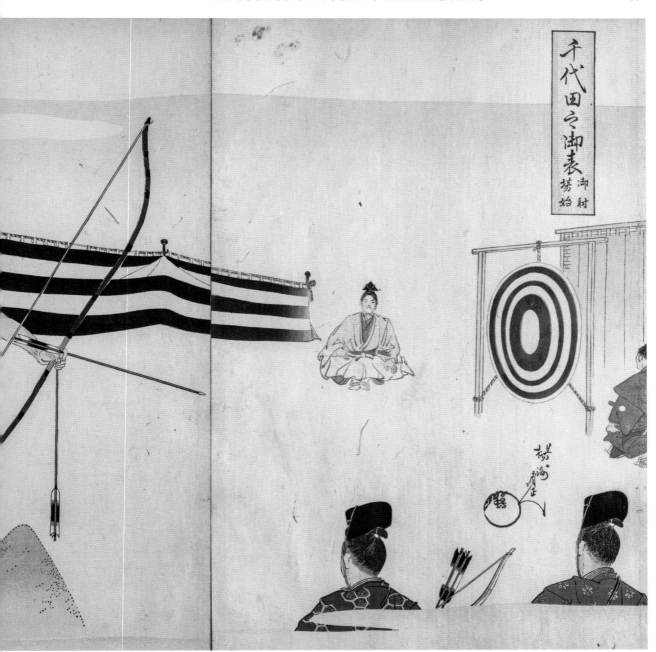

An archery (*kyudo* or *kyujutsu*) competition between samurai depicted in another print from the *Chiyoda Castle (Album of Men)* series by Yoshu Chikanobu. With few wars to fight during the Edo period, samurai who wanted to preserve their martial skills and traditions would engage in such contests with their peers.

揚州 (橋本) 周延 Yoshu (Hashimoto) Chikanobu (1838–1912)

LEFT ABOVE Detail of a print from Chikanobu's *Chiyoda Castle (Album of Women)* series titled *Ladies in Waiting of the Chiyoda Castle: Sword Practice and Puppet Kyogen* showing two women of the shogunate court practicing with what appear to be a wooden sword and *naginata*.

揚州 (橋本) 周延 Yoshu (Hashimoto) Chikanobu (1838–1912)

LEFT BELOW A woodblock print from the early 20th century titled *Fighting Lesson* by painter and printmaker Eiho Hirezaki of a man with a wooden sword and woman with a wooden *naginata* practicing in a dojo. Hirezaki's work is known for frequent portrayals of beautiful women.

鰭崎 英朋 Eiho Hirezaki (1881–1968)

BELOW Matsushita Kahei and Kinoshita Tokichiro (later known as the great unifying warlord Toyotomi Hideyoshi) dueling with swords in a print from a series *Newly Selected Records of the Taiko Hideyoshi* by Utagawa Toyonobu, dated 1883. Hideyoshi rose from peasant stock, beginning his military career under Kahei as an *ashigaru* foot soldier.

歌川 豊宣 Utagawa Toyonobu (1859–1886)

BELOW Kendo practice using bamboo *shinai* swords in an albumen silver print created from a photograph and then colored by hand, from the 1870s or 1880s, by Shinichi Suzuki, an early pioneer of Japanese photography.

真一 鈴木 Shin'ichi Suzuki (1835–1918)

BOTTOM This hand colored print, by an unidentified photographer, dated to the 1880s, shows two kendoka training on straw tatami mats. Today, kendo is nearly always practiced on wooden floors.

剣道 Kendo

Japanese archery

Kyudo archery practitioners in traditional attire at a tournament in Japan
in a photograph thought to have been taken in the 1920s. Photograph by
Michael Maslan, who spent years in Japan capturing images of sumo
wrestlers, women in kimono and scenes from everyday life.

弓道 *Kyudo*

BELOW Women wearing *hakama* practicing with *naginata* in the mid-1930s. *Naginata* was the favored weapon of female samurai and is still practiced predominantly by women in Japan today.

薙刀道 / 薙刀術 *Naginata-do / Naginatajutsu*

RIGHT ABOVE Elementary school students practicing judo in Japan during the 1910s on straw tatami mats. Mats in contemporary Japanese dojo are nearly always made from synthetic materials, but still sometimes referred to as tatami.

柔道 Judo

RIGHT BELOW Karateka performing drills in July 1947, in a photograph by John Florea. Karate had arrived in mainland Japan from Okinawa only a few decades previously, and was still largely unknown outside the country. Florea had been a combat photographer during the Pacific War and went on to have a successful career as a writer, producer and director in US television.

空手 Karate

CHAPTER 11

SAMURAI ON FILM

The bloody battles, political intrigue and human drama of the samurai era lend themselves perfectly to compelling narratives on the large and small screen. The body of samurai films and television drama, known as *jidaigeki* (period drama) is truly a rich and diverse one. It encompasses tales of unflinching loyalty, torn loyalties, betrayal, courage, giant battles, individual duels, socio-political critiques (both historical and contemporary), romance, spirituality and so much more.

Somewhat curiously, the majority of samurai films are set in the largely war-free Edo period, rather than the preceding centuries of conflict, perhaps in part due to the greater availability of records and other source material from that time. The upheavals of the period and decline of the fortunes of many samurai saw a rise in the number of master-less ronin, many of whom became wandering outcasts and therefore ideal movie heroes or anti-heroes.

One of the earliest known samurai films is Konishi Ryo's 1907 take on the kabuki play *Chushingura* (*47 Ronin*); shot with a camera in front of the stage, it is very much a recording of a theatrical production. The perennially popular tale has been filmed nearly 100 times, including a Hollywood version in 2013, starring Keanu Reeves, Hiroyuki Sanada and Tadanobu Asano. Titled *47 Ronin*, the fantasy reimagining of the classic story was visually striking but poorly received in both the US and Japan. Nevertheless, a futuristic sequel for Netflix is currently in the works. A two-part version by acclaimed director Kenji Mizoguchi in 1941 was more historically accurate but essentially a piece of wartime propaganda ordered by the government.

Japan's most celebrated and influential director, and probably the finest exponent of *jidaigeki*, Akira Kurosawa, was also forced into propaganda film-making during the war. In 1945, he made *The Men Who Tread on the Tiger's Tail*, a retelling of the escape of Minamoto no Yoshitsune and the giant monk Benkei from the shogun (Yoshitsune's brother Yoritomo). Interestingly, the film drew the ire of Japanese wartime censors while still in production for

its supposedly subversive elements, and was then banned by the American occupying authorities as part of a crackdown on the promotion of feudal and traditional values. It was finally released in 1953, a year after the occupation ended. By that time, Kurosawa had already brought Japanese filmmaking, the samurai movie and his go-to leading man Toshiro Mifune to the attention of the world with *Rashomon* (1950), winner of the Golden Lion at Venice Film

Festival and an honorary Oscar.

In 1954, Kurosawa released what is still to be found near the top of most rankings of the greatest films of all time. The epic *Seven Samurai* influenced directors worldwide, was remade as *The Magnificent Seven* and laid down the blueprint for the "putting the team together" sequence that has become an action movie trope. Instruction in sword fighting and its choreography was handled by Yoshio Sugino, a sensei from Tenshin Shoden Katori Shinto-ryu who brought a level of authenticity to the battle scenes very different from the kabuki-inspired theatrics of earlier samurai productions. Sugino, also an accomplished judoka and aikidoka, became personal budo sensei to Mifune, star of 16 Kurosawa films, many of which Sugino also choreographed.

Kurosawa's *The Hidden Fortress* (1958) famously inspired the original *Star Wars* (in which Mifune was reportedly offered a part), while the plot of *Yojimbo* (1961) was so obviously plundered for Sergio Leone's classic Spaghetti Western *A Fistful of Dollars* that its release was delayed for years over the ensuing legal wrangle.

Mifune eventually appeared in more than 150 films (not all *jidaigeki*) and redefined the on-screen samurai with his numerous iconic portrayals of often uncouth *bushi*. In the same year as *Seven Samurai*, Mifune starred in Hiroshi Inagaki's *Musashi Miyamoto*, which won an honorary Oscar and was the first of a trilogy loosely based on the life of the legendary swordsman. Though the partnership was not as significant as Mifune's one with Kurosawa, he and Inagaki teamed up for a number of other *jidaigeki* during the 1950s and early 1960s, a period known as the golden age of samurai films and Japanese cinema as a whole.

As it did across much of the world, the rise of television led to a plunge in cinema-going in Japan. From more than a billion annual admissions in the late 1950s, total audiences were down to less than a fifth of that by the early 1970s. *Jidaigeki* suffered particularly badly as audiences appeared to grow weary of the genre and yakuza gangster. Erotic films

47 Ronin (2013) transported the Ako Jiken tale of revenge by master-less samurai for their fallen lord to a fantasy world of magic and monsters for this Hollywood take on this most-filmed of all *bushi* stories.

四十七浪人 *Shijushichi Ronin*

and other fare came to the fore. Samurai never completely disappeared from the screens though and highlights from the period include the six *Lone Wolf and Cub* (*Kozure Okami*) films based on a seminal and influential manga, which also became a hit television series.

1980 saw the release of one of the outstanding films that was set in the Sengoku period, Kurosawa's *Kagemusha*, winner of the Palme d'Or at Cannes. Funded with help from George Lucas and Francis Ford Coppola, the three-hour epic culminates with the Battle of Nagashino, though large sections of its battle scenes featuring thousands of extras were cut from the final version by Kurosawa himself. Protagonists included Takeda Shingen, Uesugi Kenshin, Oda Nobunaga and Tokugawa Ieyasu.

Takeda Shingen and Uesugi Kenshin faced off in another big-budget production, Haruki Kadokawa's *Heaven and Earth* 10 years later, kicking off another decade that would prove to be a relatively barren one for samurai film.

Since the turn of the millennium, the genre has enjoyed something of a renaissance, with veteran director Yoji Yamada's samurai trilogy (2002–2006) achieving both commercial and critical success, including an Oscar nomination for *The Twilight Samurai*.

In 2003, Yojiro Takita's *When the Last Sword is Drawn* also won awards and critical praise for its tale of two samurai with torn loyalties at the end of the Edo period, but failed to even cover its production costs at the domestic box office. Takita would go on to a surprise foreign language Oscar win in 2009 for his contemporary film *Departures*, Japan's first

victory in the category since *Samurai I: Miyamoto Musashi* and its only since it became an official award.

2003 also saw another take on the *Zatoichi* blind swordsman story, this time written, directed by and starring Kitano "Beat" Takeshi, which enjoyed considerable commercial success and won the Silver Lion at Venice. The character has appeared in more than 25 films, including a 1970 crossover *Zatoichi Meets Yojimbo* starring Mifune.

The prolific Takashi Miike has turned his hand to the genre, most notably with two remakes of 1960s films. *13 Assassins* (2010) is a gory bloodbath of a revenge film and exactly what might be expected from a Miike samurai film. His 3D remake of *Harakiri*, titled *Hara-Kiri: Death of a Samurai* (2011), is more measured but features a long, truly gut-wrenching scene of seppuku with a bamboo sword. The story is based around a practice by impoverished samurai who would visit a lord and ask for permission to commit hara-kiri in their courtyard, usually to be given some money and sent on their way. The premise of the films is the bluff of the samurai, who in this case has pawned his real swords, being called.

Not all *jidaigeki* are deadly serious, even some of those about real dramatic events have been given comedy touches. *The Floating Castle* (2012), co-directed by Isshin Inudo and Shinji Higuchi, recounts the Siege of Oshi during Toyotomi Hideyoshi's unification war, where a vastly outnumbered force defends the castle. There are plenty of light-hearted moments in the film, though the use of dams to flood the defenders led to its release being delayed after the giant tsunami of 2011, out of respect for the victims and survivors. Inudo directed 2019's *Samurai Shifters* (*Hikkoshi Daimyo*), a comedy based on the Edo era practice of moving daimyo and their entire clan from one domain to another in order to keep them too weak to rebel or to settle scores. The film is notable for multiple references to homosexuality between samurai and the cause of friction between two senior *bushi* is spurned romantic advances.

BUSHI ON THE BOX

The first *jidaigeki* series to gain a following outside Japan was *Onmitsu Kenshi* (*Spy Swordsman*), which debuted in 1962. The irreverent stories of a ronin and his ninja allies were an unexpected hit among young viewers in Australia when they began screening in 1964, though its success was not repeated elsewhere.

It is impossible to talk about samurai television series (also known as *jidaigeki*) without mentioning public broadcaster NHK's year-long Taiga dramas. These big-budget productions featuring star casts have run annually since 1963 and have probably done more to familiarize ordinary Japanese with the age of the samurai than school history lessons. *Date Masamune: The One-Eyed Dragon* (1987) starring Ken Watanabe as Date Masamune helped launch the career of Watanabe, who later came to the attention of Western audiences alongside Tom Cruise in *The Last Samurai*. The 2020 Taiga drama *Kirin ga Kuru* was the first to be shot in 4K and the most watched of recent years.

Not all of NHK's *jidaigeki* were Taiga dramas, such as the acclaimed *Sanada Taiheiki* (45 episodes from 1985 to 1986), which followed the fortunes of the Sanada clan and the ninja who worked for them at the end of Sengoku period.

There have naturally been numerous samurai dramas from Japan's commercial broadcasters, including many adapted from films, novels and manga. Kinji Fukasaku's *Shogun's Samurai* (1978), about a succession battle within the Tokugawa shogunate, was turned into a 39-part series *The Yagyu Conspiracy*. The film also starred Shinichi "Sonny" Chiba and Hiroyuki Sanada.

American network NBC's *Shogun* miniseries aired in 1980 in the US and boosted interest in samurai and Japan in general in the West. Adapted from James Clavell's novel, it was very loosely based on the adventures of a shipwrecked English sailor at the turn of the 17th century and featured Mifune as a Tokugawa Ieyasu-like character. The series was less well received in Japan when it was broadcast the following year and may have contributed to NHK making a Taiga drama about Ieyasu in 1981.

LEFT A ukiyo-e woodblock print part of the triptych *Minamoto no Yoshitsune fights Benkei on Gojo Bridge* by Kuniyoshi. This scene depicts the duel which would result in Benkei becoming the young Minamoto's protector and friend. Here the giant is attacked by a *tengu* demon, one of the creatures that according to legends about Yoshitsune, were said to have trained him in combat during his youth and that on this occasion rush to his aid.

歌川 国芳 Utagawa Kuniyoshi (1798–1861)

ABOVE *The Men Who Tread on the Tiger's Tail* (1945) was Akira Kurosawa's telling of some of the exploits of Minamoto no Yoshitsune and his faithful attendant Benkei, which have been the subject of numerous plays, books, TV series and films.

虎の尾を踏む男達 *Tora no o wo fumu otokotachi*

Rashomon (1950) did nothing less than put Japanese cinema on the map. Directed by Akira Kurosawa and starring Toshiro Mifune, the seminal *Rashomon* depicted the same short incident from the differing perspectives of four characters. The movie was based on two short stories by Ryunosuke Akutagawa and set outside Kyoto during the chaos of the 12th century as powerful samurai clans battled for supremacy against the backdrop of an enfeebled government. Machiko Kyo starred as the wife of a samurai with Toshiro Mifune as a manic bandit.

羅生門 *Rashomon*

A poster trumpeting *Rashomon* success as the first Japanese
film to win the Golden Lion at Venice film festival and an
honorary Academy Award (the best foreign language film
category was yet to be officially established).

羅生門 *Rashomon*

Seven Samurai (1954) united Kurosawa and Mifune again for this hugely influential epic production about villagers that recruit a ragtag band of ronin to protect them from bandits is hailed to this day as a masterpiece of filmmaking.

七人の侍 *Shichinin no samurai*

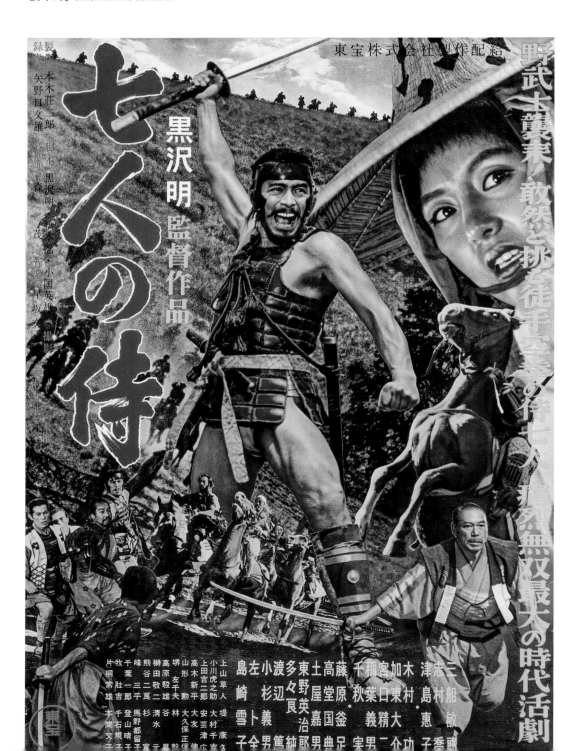

Mifune's Kikuchiyo, a temperamental but humorous character of the kind the actor portrayed so consummately, turns out to be the one member of the seven who is not actually a samurai. The three and a half hour film set in the late 16th century cemented Kurosawa's international reputation as Japan's finest director.

七人の侍 *Shichinin no samurai*

LEFT *Samurai II: Duel at Ichijoji Temple* (1955) starred Toshiro Mifune in the second of Hiroshi Inagaki's trilogy about the storied swordsman Miyamoto Musashi. The film was adapted from Eiji Yoshikawa's novel *Musashi*, which did much to popularize, and embellish, his legend in Japan.

続宮本武蔵・一乗寺の決闘 *Zoku Miyamoto Musashi: Ichijoji no Ketto*

BELOW *Shin Heike Monogatari* (1955) has no official English title, but translates as *New Tale of Heike*, and was based on a poem that recounts the battles for supremacy between the Taira and Minamoto clans. It was an early example of a color samurai film and a relatively rare foray into the genre for legendary director Kenji Mizoguchi.

新・平家物語 *Shin Heike Monogatari*

TOP *Throne of Blood* (1957) was Kurosawa's retelling of *Macbeth*, transported to the samurai era. The fear in Toshiro Mifune's eyes in this scene is at least partly real as the arrows were also real, shot by members of a university *kyudo* archery club. Many of the actors who were supposed to shoot arrows were too scared to do so.

蜘蛛巣城 *Kumonosu-jo*

ABOVE *Yojimbo* (1961) is another acclaimed film by Kurosawa starring Mifune, this time as a crude but shrewd masterless samurai (ronin) who plays two gangs which are terrifying a town off of each other. The title translates as "bodyguard."

用心棒 *Yojimbo*

Sanjuro (1962) was Kurosawa's sequel to his hit of the previous year *Yojimbo*, with Mifune reprising his role as a pragmatic and unheroic ronin, both films showcased the director's often overlooked comedic side.

椿三十郎 *Tsubaki Sanjuro*

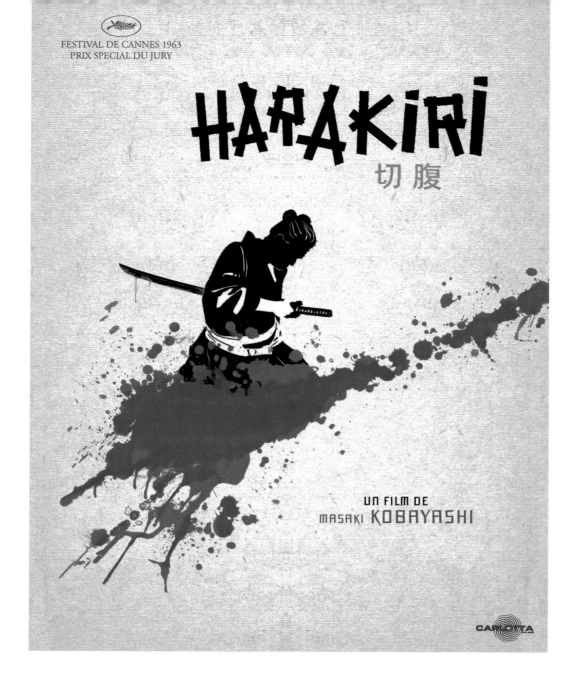

FESTIVAL DE CANNES 1963
PRIX SPECIAL DU JURY

HARAKIRI

切腹

UN FILM DE
MASAKI KOBAYASHI

ABOVE *Harakiri* (1962) by Masaki Kobayashi won the Special Jury Award at Cannes Film Festival the following year for this layered story of an impoverished ronin who asks to commit ritual suicide in the grounds of a lord's palace. Takashi Miike's 2011 remake also premiered at Cannes.

切腹 *Seppuku*

RIGHT ABOVE • レッド・サン *Red Sun* (1971) was a Spaghetti Western by Terence Young (director of three James Bond films) featuring Toshiro Mifune, alongside Charles Bronson, Alain Delon and Ursula Andress, as the samurai bodyguard of the Japanese ambassador to the US.

RIGHT BELOW *Portrait of a Samurai* a painting by Dutch artist Overmer Fisshel from an exhibition at the Tokyo National Museum. The attire appears identical to that of Mifune in *Red Sun* and may have inspired the costume designer.

武士の肖像 *Bushi no shozo*

Een Japanner in zijn Asa Kamisimo of plegtgewaad.

ABOVE *Lone Wolf And Cub: Baby Cart To Hades*
(1972) with Wakayama Tomisaburo, and Tomikawa
Akihiro as his infant son. *Lone Wolf and Cub (Kozure
Okami)* was a series of six films (four released in
1972) about a disgraced ronin played by
Wakayama traveling the land with his son.

子連れ狼・死に風に向う乳母車 *Kozure Okami:
Shinikazeni mukau ubaguruma*

RIGHT Based on an acclaimed manga, the first
three films were directed by Kenji Misumi, while
Wakayama Tomisaburo produced the remaining
three with a different director for each.

子連れ狼 *Kozure Okami*

ABOVE *Kagemusha* (1980) was a triumphant return for Kurosawa after a miserable decade for the director during which he attempted to take his own life. The story of a petty thief who is forced to impersonate the daimyo Takeda Shingen—the title means "shadow warrior"—was a commercial and critical hit.

影武者 *Kagemusha*

LEFT *Takeda Daizen Daibu Harunobu Nyudo Shingen— Ready for Battle at Kawanakajima in Shinano Province in the Eleventh Month of 1553*, a print by Utagawa Kuniyoshi from the 1840s. Takeda Shingen was played by Tatsuya Nakadai in Kurosawa's *Kagemusha* (1980).

歌川 国芳 Utagawa Kuniyoshi (1798–1861)

Ran (1985): another epic-scale production from Kurosawa set in the Sengoku period, it was inspired by Shakespeare's *King Lear* and legends of the daimyo Mori Motonari. Though Kurosawa went on to make other films, *Ran*, the biggest-budget Japanese film at the time, can be seen as his true swansong.

乱 *Ran*

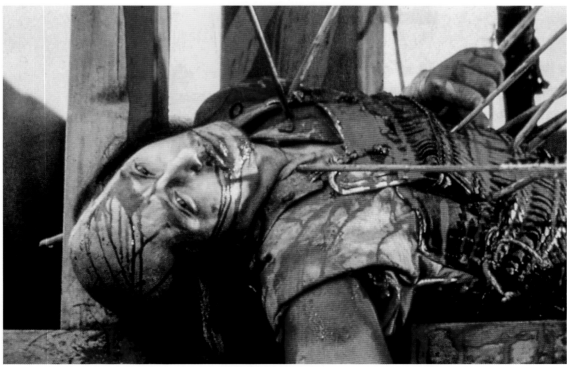

BELOW AND BOTTOM *The Last Samurai* (2003) was inspired by the events of the Satsuma Rebellion in 1877 (below, a print which is part of a triptych by Yoshitoshi entitled *Battle around Kumamoto Castle*), when disaffected *bushi* led by Saigo Takamori, unhappy at the direction the nation was headed in and what they saw as excessive westernization, took up arms against the new Meiji government. They were destroyed by a vastly larger and better equipped army in what was truly the last stand of the samurai.

大蘇 (月岡) 芳年 Taiso (Tsukioka) Yoshitoshi (1839–1892)

RIGHT Despite shooting much of it in New Zealand and making Tom Cruise the star and his fictional character the hero, Edward Zwick's film, *The Last Samurai,* based very loosely on historical events was well received in Japan, taking over $130 million at the box office there. The strong Japanese cast of Ken Watanabe, Hiroyuki Sanada and Koyuki Kato, and lavish production values, made it the biggest imported hit of the year.

ラスト サムライ *The Last Samurai*

13 Assassins (2010) saw Takashi Miike remake Eiichi Kudo's acclaimed 1963 film with a bigger budget, more on-screen bloodshed and the stylized violence the director is so adept at. A group of samurai, led by Yakusho Koji, are assigned to kill a psychopathic lord, culminating in one of the most compelling climactic battles in samurai film history.

十三人の刺客 *Jusannin no Shikaku*

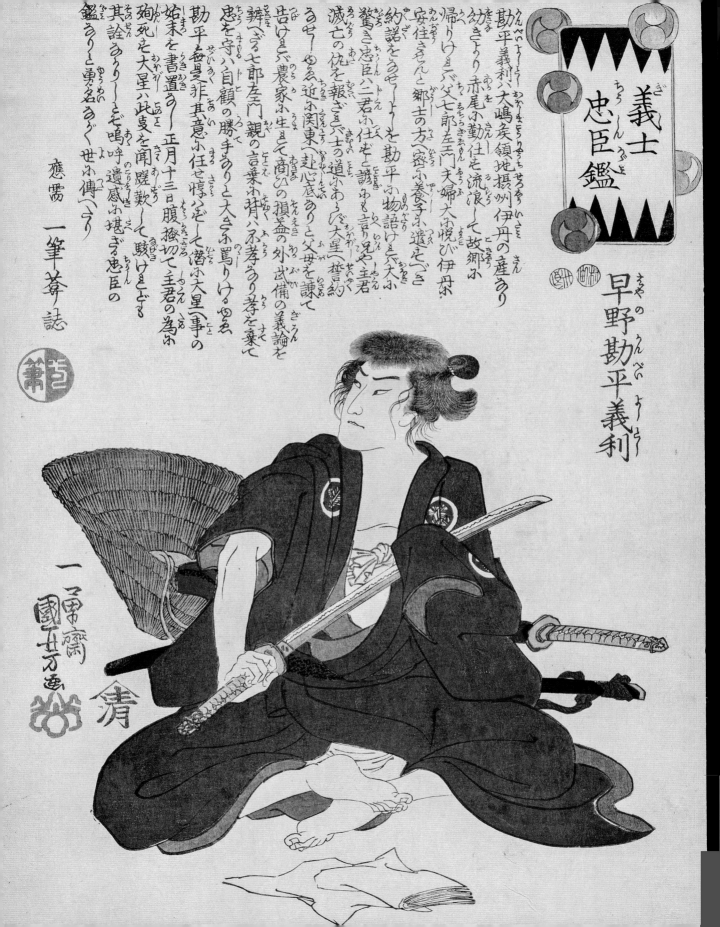

義士
忠臣鑑

早野勘平義利

勘平義利ハ大嶋の領地摂州伊丹の産なり
幼きよりと赤尾小勤仕を流浪して故郷ふ
帰りけるがバ父七郎左三門夫婦大ふ悦び伊丹ふ
安住さきんと郷士の方へ密ふ養子ふ遣そべき
約諾をなもとーーを勘平ふ物語けるを大ふ
驚き忠臣ハ二君ふ仕ぜと誠ふ言ひ況や主君
滅亡の仇を報ざるバ士の道ふあらべと大星(誓約
るせーーめ迄近小関東へ赴心底ありと父母を諫て
告けるふ農家小生まて商ひの損益の外武備の義論を
辨へざる七郎左門親の言葉ふ背ハ不孝なり孝を棄て
忠を守ハ自領の勝手なりと大きふ罵りける
勘平毫毛非其意ふ任せ惇だーーて潜ふ大星(事の
始末を書置り一正月十三日腹掻切て主君の為ふ
殉死をと大星八此曳を南膾歎して駿けとどる
其詮ありーーとぞ鳴呼遺感ふ堪ざる忠臣の
鑑ありと勇名るぐ世ふ傳へり

應需　一筆菴誌

一勇斎
國芳画

LEFT A print of Hayano Kanpei Yoshitoshi preparing to commit seppuku. The character is based on Kayano Sanpei, one of the retainers of Lord Asano, the samurai forced to commit seppuku by the Tokugawa shogunate in the 47 Ronin incident. Names were changed slightly in the plays and stories based on the incident to avoid censorship by the shogunate, so Kayano Sanpei becomes Hayano Kanpei.

歌川 国芳 Utagawa Kuniyoshi (1798–1861)

TOP AND ABOVE *Hara-Kiri: Death of a Samurai* (*Ichimei*, 2011): another remake of a classic by Miike, again featuring Yakusho Koji. Starring kabuki actor Ichikawa Ebizo and with a score by Ryuichi Sakamoto, the carefully paced narrative questions the honor and humanity of the Bushido code.

一命 *Ichimei*

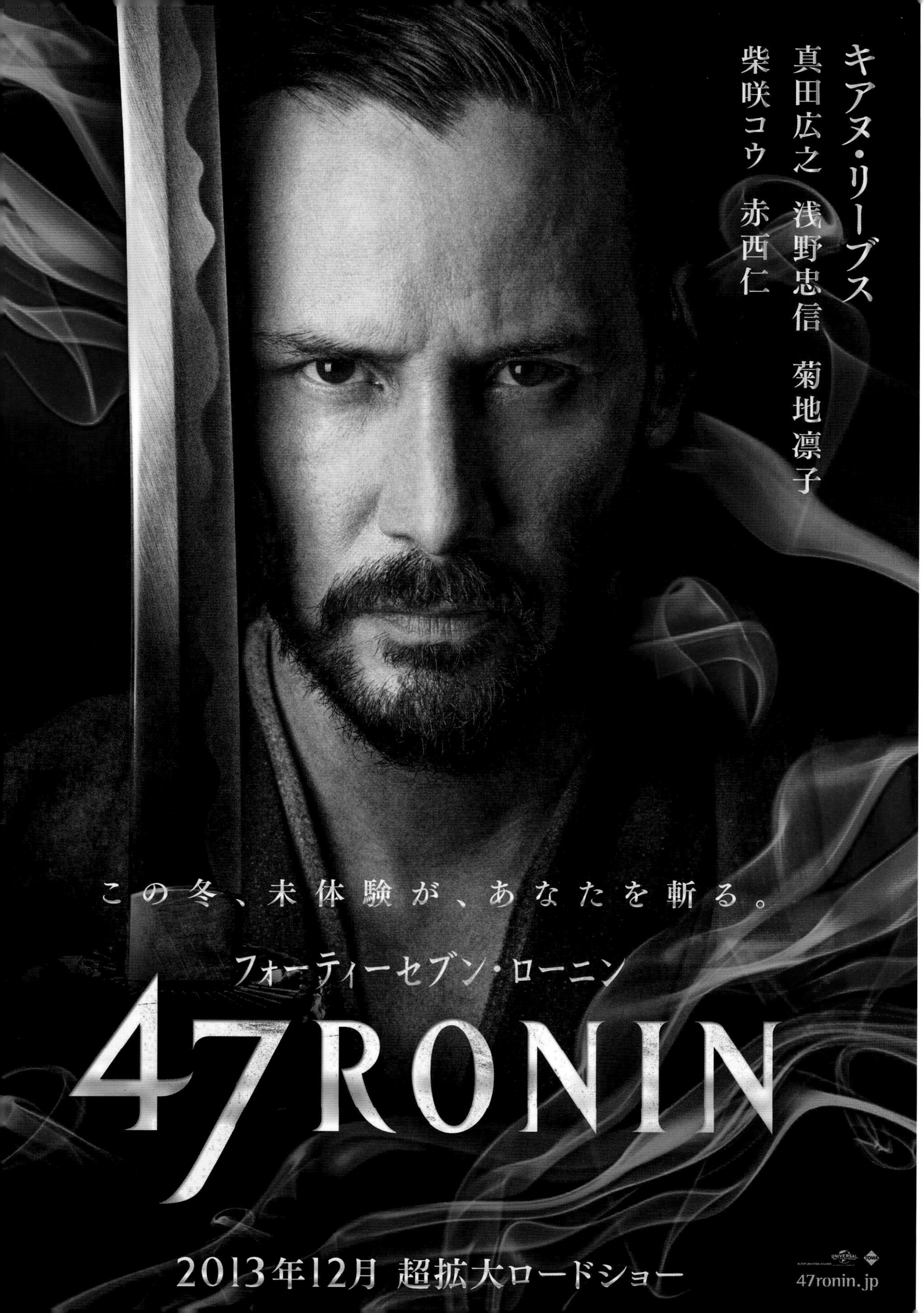

キアヌ・リーブス
真田広之　浅野忠信　菊地凛子
柴咲コウ　赤西仁

この冬、未体験が、あなたを斬る。

フォーティーセブン・ローニン

47RONIN

2013年12月　超拡大ロードショー

47ronin.jp

47 Ronin (2013) the directorial debut of Carl Rinsch, starred Keanu Reeves as a half-Japanese character created for the film. The film failed to cover its big production budget worldwide and did not go down well in Japan. The Japanese poster uses the English name for the film, also written in the katakana script for foreign words, and does not mention *Chushingura*, the name by which the story is most known in Japan.

四十七浪人 *Shijushichi Ronin*

47 Ronin was visually impressive and featured a strong Japanese cast of Hiroyuki Sanada, Tadanobu Asano, Rinko Kikuchi and Ko Shibasaki, but was not well received by critics or audiences. In the image (right), a giant played by the late Neil Fingleton, is about to destroy one of the 47 Ronin.

四十七浪人 *Shijushichi Ronin*

CHAPTER 12

THE SAMURAI IN MANGA, ANIME AND VIDEO GAMES

The same qualities which make samurai tales so suited to adaptation into films and television also make them an ideal basis for manga, anime and videogames. There is a huge amount of crossover between the formats, with a significant number of stories making appearances across multiple media. This is not peculiar to samurai franchises, but common with many genres in Japan.

The word manga comprised of two characters, which can be read as "unrestricted image," giving a clue to the nature of the approach to the medium of many of its creators. This freewheeling take on storytelling is reflected in many samurai manga, which include fictional narratives set against the background of real events, alternative histories, relatively faithful historical accounts and even *bushi* transported into science-fiction scenarios.

This flexible approach is apparent in *Koga Ninpocho*, the story of 10 ninja from the Koga and Iga clans who are drawn into a succession conflict by Tokugawa Ieyasu, with each representing one of the shogun's grandsons. The battle to decide who will rule for the next millennium is complicated by the fact that the heirs of the two ninja clans are in love. The story is based on a 1959 novel, which was made into manga in 1963 and 2003, an anime series in 2005, and a successful live-action film the same year, a typical media-crossing path for Japanese franchises.

The *Lone Wolf and Cub* (*Kozure Okami*) stories, discussed in the film and television chapter, began life as a manga by Kazuo Koike that went on to exert an influence on Western comics, music and movies. The tale of a former executioner who is forced to wander the land with his young son after he is unfairly exiled has won praise for its philosophical examination of father-son bonds, the human condition, martial arts, politics, religion and more.

Koike also wrote *Lady Snowblood* (*Shurayuki-hime*), which also became an early 1970s live-action film. The titular character uses her sexuality to lure her victims as she seeks revenge on those who destroyed her family, often using a katana concealed inside a traditional Japanese umbrella. The story was transported to a post-apocalyptic world for a 2001 feature film, *The Princess Blade*, with the same Japanese title as the original.

Rurouni Kenshin is another story which has made the journey across several media. Set at the end of the beginning of the Meiji period, it follows the adventures of a former killer who has forsworn violence, carries a sword with a blunt edge where the blade should be and attempts to atone for his previous sins. The manga, which ran from the mid to late 90s, has sold more than 70 million copies. It was also made into an anime series, two anime films, a number of video games and a trilogy of live-action films in the 2010s which took more than $160 million at the box office. Two more live-action films were in the pipeline at the time of writing.

The path from manga to anime to live-action film (the 100th directed by Takashi Miike) was also trodden by *Blade of the Immortal* (*Mugen no Junin*), the story of a ronin cursed with immortality until he kills 1,000 evildoers. His immortality is ensured by special worms which heal his wounds and even reattach severed limbs, a touch of the magical-realism not uncommon in samurai manga. Created by Hiroaki Samura, the series ran from 1993 to 2012.

Afro Samurai, as the name might suggests, also takes some historical liberties, with a futuristic story featuring a weed-smoking samurai heavily influenced by creator Takashi Okazaki's love of US hip-hop culture. Starting life in a *dojinshi* (self-published/amateur) magazine, *Afro Samurai* spawned an anime series and feature film, the latter voiced by Samuel L. Jackson and Lucy Liu, and both featuring a sound–track from RZA of martial arts-loving hip-hop collective Wu-Tang Clan.

Multi-media, genre-bending franchise *Gin Tama* is another science-fiction samurai tale, one of an invasion of feudal Japan by aliens who ban swords. This best-selling manga has been accompanied by successful anime series, anime films, live-action films, light novels and video games. *Gin Tama* is acclaimed for its quirky storylines, striking visuals and comedic touches.

Somewhat more grounded in reality, the life of legendary swordsman Miyamoto Musashi, or at least a version of it, was told in the influential *Vagabond* manga written and illustrated by Takehiko Inoue between 1999 and 2015. The action begins after the Battle of Sekigahara, in which a young Musashi is reported to have fought on the losing side against the Tokugawa clan. The acclaimed series, which has sold more than 80 million copies, follows Musashi's journey through life as he shifts from his quest to be an invincible warrior to one of self-discovery.

In a similar vein of largely fictional narrative against the backdrop of real events, *Angolmois: Record of Mongol Invasion* (*Angorumoa: Genko Kassenki*), tells of prisoners exiled to Tsushima to help defend the island against the first Mongol invasion attempt. Running from 2013 to 2018, an anime series began broadcasting as the manga was coming to an end.

Not all anime are based on manga, and the oldest extant Japanese animated film happens to feature a samurai. *The Dull Sword* (*Namakura Gatana*) is four-minute comedy about a hapless samurai tricked into buying a blunt katana and subsequently losing the fights he uses it in. It was released in 1917 and thought lost until a copy was discovered in a second-hand shop by a university professor in Osaka in 2007.

Kurosawa's *Seven Samurai* was given an imaginative anime reinterpretation exactly half a century after its release with Toshifumi Takizawa's *Samurai 7* (2004), which transposed to a futuristic world the story of a group of villagers hiring a ragtag bunch of *bushi* to protect them against bandits. The same year, director Shinichiro Watanabe followed up his much-lauded genre-busting *Cowboy Bebop* anime with *Samurai Champloo*, another style-bending series. Set in a parallel Edo period, the 26 episodes (the standard length for anime series) are infused with hip-hop style as they follow the trials and tribulations of two swordsmen on a quest to help a waitress locate a mysterious samurai. Against the backdrop of historical reality, the stories weave in breakdancing and graffiti, while featuring characters ranging from Miyamoto Musashi to an American baseball team.

Intrigue in the Bakumatsu—Irohanihoheto sticks

closer to history, though blends the supernatural into its alternative take on the final years of the Edo period (known as the Bakumatsu) and includes figures such as Saigo Takamori and Sakamoto Ryoma. The 2006–2007 series is also notable for being one of the earliest acclaimed original anime samurai productions to have bowed on an internet streaming platform.

There are actually a relatively small number of original—not based on an anime series, manga or other source material—animated samurai feature films. One such production is 2007's *Sword of the Stranger* (*Sutorenjia Mukohadan*), an anime feature directed by Masahiro Ando. Set in the Sengoku period, it tells of an orphan boy who hires a ronin to protect him and his dog, from assassins sent to kill him from Ming China. The blend of comedy, complex plot and some gory action won the film fans both at home and abroad, and saw it submitted to the 2009 Oscars, nominated for other awards, and screened at international film festivals.

One genuinely multimedia samurai franchise is *Sengoku Basara*, which started life as an all-action fighting video game. Created by Hiroyuki Kobayashi, the first game was released for the PlayStation 2 in 2005 and the series features characters from the turbulent times when warlords battled to unify the

country, including Oda Nobunaga, Date Masamune, Uesugi Kenshin, Takeda Shingen and Tokugawa Ieyasu. In addition to more than a dozen games, the *Sengoku Basara* realm has spread out into manga, anime, a live-action TV series, radio shows and theatrical plays. The Takarazuka Revue, a celebrated all-female troupe, even produced a musical version that ran for a year.

Naturally enough, fighting games account for a large proportion of samurai titles, with most being centered on individual combat, plus the occasional strategy game in which entire armies are controlled. One particularly expansive one-on-one combat series is *Samurai Shodown* (*Samurai Spirits*), which has run to more than 20 games across multiple consoles, PC and arcade versions from 1993 to 2020. Set in the 18th century, the protagonists are a mix of historical figures, mythical monsters and fictional Western characters.

Way of the Samurai (*Samurai*) is another long-running series, with the first appearing in 2002 and the latest spin-off game released in 2020. The games have won plaudits for their in-depth plots outside the fighting sequences, which span the samurai era from the 15th to 19th centuries. As with samurai anime and manga, in video games, traditional elements are freely merged with out-of-place modern touches. The

Captured from PlayStation®4 Pro. 4k images require a 4k display.

best-selling late 90s *Bushido Blade* series incorporated the samurai's semi-mythical code of honor into gameplay by punishing players for ignoble behavior, but also featured a helipad.

Fate/Grand Order is a smartphone game that features multiple samurai characters, including some based on historical figures, though not strictly samurai franchise. First launched in Japan in July 2015 by Aniplex, a Sony subsidiary known for anime, various incarnations have raked in billions of dollars worldwide since. It has gone on to spawn a hit arcade version, anime series and films, manga and stage plays.

Not all samurai games originated in Japan, a notable example being the two *Shogun: Total War* battle strategy games developed by British company The Creative Assembly. An early PC strategy title was 1989's *Sword of the Samurai* from a US publisher; re-released in 2014, it is known for its historical accuracy in portraying the wars of unification. Meanwhile, German developer Mimimi Games was behind *Shadow Tactics: Blades of the Shogun*, a highly-rated "stealth" tactics game set in an alternative Edo period, with an emphasis on evading enemies rather than open combat.

Video game graphics have advanced rapidly in recent years, with the best of them now displaying levels of artistry once more commonly found in films.

With acknowledged inspiration by films such as *Seven Samurai*, *Ghost of Tsushima* features a "Kurosawa mode" allowing players to experience a throwback to classic *jidaigeki* cinema.

Such sophistication is to be found in *Sekiro: Shadows Die Twice* an award-winning 2019 action-adventure game in which players control a wandering *shinobi* (ninja) in a semi-fictional late Sengoku era.

More stunning visuals can be found in *Nioh 2*, a 2020 prequel to the first title in the series, another game set in the Sengoku period which incorporates supernatural elements into its complex role-playing action.

July 2020 saw the release of the highly-anticipated *Ghost of Tsushima*, an action-adventure title for the PlayStation 4 set during the 1274 Mongol invasion. Developed by US-based Sony studio Sucker Punch Productions, the game won plaudits for its stunning visuals, attention to historical detail and expansive world, selling 2.4 million copies in the first three days of release.

ABOVE *Koga Ninpocho* 甲賀忍法帖
The cover of the first *The Kouga Ninja Scrolls*
(*Koga Ninpocho*, 1963) manga by Haruo
Koyama, based on an earlier novel by Yamada
Futaro, it went on to spawn an anime series, a
movie, more novels and more manga versions.

RIGHT *Lone Wolf and Cub* 子連れ狼
Panels from the English version of the *Lone Wolf
and Cub* (*Kozure Okami*) manga by author Kazuo
Koike and artist Goseki Kojima. The manga ran
from 1970 to 1976, became a hit live-action TV
and film series, and influenced numerous
creators of comics, films and television in the US.

Demon Slayer Vol. 1 鬼滅の刃
Cover and panels from the English edition of the first
volume of *Demon Slayer* (*Kimetsu no Yaiba*) by Koyoharu
Gotouge, which ran from 2016 to 2020. Though set in the
early 20th century, the young hero wields a katana with a
blade (*yaiba*) made from a magical material.

Demon Slayer Vol. 7 and 8 鬼滅の刃
Covers of the English editions of volumes 7 and 8 of *Demon Slayer*, which became a multi-billion dollar franchise, with sales of more then 150 million copies of the manga, an acclaimed anime series and record-breaking anime film.

Demon Slayer Vol. 8 鬼滅の刃
Panels from the English edition of volume 8 of *Demon Slayer*. The Demon Slayer: Kimetsu no Yaiba the Movie: Mugen Train (*Gekijo-ban "Kimetsu no Yaiba" Mugen Ressha-hen*) movie by Haruo Sotozaki took more than $430 million worldwide, becoming the highest-grossing Japanese film in history, despite being released during the 2020 pandemic.

LEFT TOP *Gintama Vol. 1 and 53* 銀魂
Covers of the Italian editions of volumes 1 and 53 of *Gintama* (2003–2019) by Hideaki Sorachi, a sci-fi samurai tale that expanded into a multi-media franchise of anime series, anime and live-action films, video games and novels.

LEFT BOTTOM *Gintama Vol. 53* 銀魂
Panels from *Gintama* volume 53. The best-selling manga won plaudits for its offbeat humor and storylines based around an alien invasion of a parallel Edo period world where swords are confiscated by the invaders.

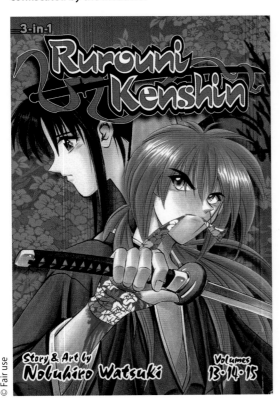

© Fair use

ABOVE AND RIGHT *Rurouni Kenshin Vol. 13, 14, 15*
るろうに剣心
Cover and panels from a combined English edition of volumes 13, 14 and 15 of *Rurouni Kenshin* (1994–1999). The story of a former assassin who wields a blunted blade to avoid further killing was made into anime series and films, video games and a series of box-office hit live-action films that launched in 2012.

© Fair use

© Fair use

LEFT TOP AND BOTTOM The *Ishi-jo, wife of Oboshi Yoshio* print by Utagawa Kuniyoshi shows the wife of the leader of the 47 Ronin wielding a *naginata*. From the *Biographies of Loyal and Righteous Hearts* series. Bottom left is Katsukawa Shunei's print *The Second Ichikawa Monnosuke as a Man Dressed in a Kimono* from 1793, showing a famous kabuki actor Ichikawa Monnosuke II (1743–1794) dressed for a part.

歌川 国芳 Utagawa Kuniyoshi (1798–1861) and
勝川 春英 Katsukawa Shunei (1762–1819)

RIGHT TOP AND BOTTOM *Animal Crossing* どうぶつの森 is a series of open-ended social simulation Nintendo video games that debuted in 2001. The 2020 *Animal Crossing: New Horizons* was a record-setting hit that allows players to create their own characters. These two characters, created by Bramble's Crossing, are based on ukiyo-e samurai prints by Utagawa Kuniyoshi and Katsukawa Shunei, respectively.

BELOW *Sengoku Basara* 戦国 BASARA
is a popular multi-media franchise that began life as
a video game in 2005. It features many of the
leading figures from the Sengoku era, including
Date Masamune, the "One-Eyed Dragon of Oshu,"
pictured here alongside Sanada Yukimura, another
legendary samurai, who has his own dedicated
game in the series.

ABOVE *Sengoku Basara* 戦国 BASARA 4
Sengoku BASARA 4 came out in 2015 for the
PlayStation 3, continuing the tradition of the
fighting game series very loosely based on
historical events. In Japan, the game held
collaborative promotions campaigns with the
movie *47 Ronin* starring Keanu Reeves.

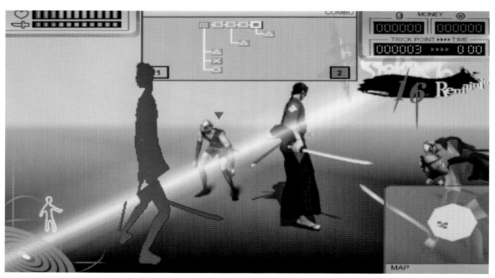

LEFT TOP *Way of the Samurai* (侍) from developer Acquire was released for the PlayStation 2 in 2002, and was followed by sequel games for later consoles. The games won acclaim for their action and complex plots spanning the era of the samurai.

LEFT MIDDLE *Samurai Champloo: Sidetracked* (サムライチャンプル 一) is a fighting game released in 2006 for the PlayStation 2 and inspired by the cult hit *Samurai Champloo* anime. Though it was largely unrelated to the source material, the game retained the hip-hop influences and Edo period setting.

LEFT BOTTOM *Bushido Blade* (ブシドーブレード) was one of the earliest samurai games, though set in the modern era, released for the PlayStation 1 in 1997. It differs from most fighting games in its more realistic combat gameplay, where a single strike can kill.

ABOVE *Samurai Shodown* (サムライスピリッツ) titled *Samurai Spirits* in Japan, is one of the longest-running series of the genre, with numerous games released for various consoles and arcade versions released between 1993 and 2020. The fighting game set in the 18th century and featuring some historical figures, also has spin-off manga, anime series and film, and trading cards.

BELOW A ukiyo-e print by Utagawa Kuniyoshi titled *Morozumi Bungo-no-kami Masakiyo, One of Three Heroic Deaths in Battle*, from the series *Courageous Generals of Kai and Echigo Provinces: The Twenty-four Generals of the Takeda Clan*, dated to the mid-19th century. The influence of the print by Kuniyoshi, a ukiyo-e master, on the image on the right is clear to see.

歌川 国芳 Utagawa Kuniyoshi (1798–1861)

ABOVE *Infestation*
Based on the *Metroid* series of Nintendo action-adventure games, this print by Jed Henry is entitled *Infestation*. The print is not only influenced by ukiyo-e, but created from traditional woodblock printing techniques in a workshop in Tokyo. The artist specializes in images of contemporary Japanese pop culture expressed through the medium of ukiyo-e.

RIGHT *The Queen*
This ukiyo-e print *The Queen* by contemporary artist Jed Henry is also based on the *Metroid* game series. Some elements from the suit of armor in the image below are visible in the print, including the sode shoulder guards, the breastplate, the *kusazuri* thigh protectors and the *suneate* shin guards.

LEFT A suit of 18th century *gusoku* armor with a helmet crest or *maedate* featuring a copper moon adorned with silver waves. The *kusazuri* plates that hang from the breastplate protect the lower torso and thighs, while the *haidate* plates that begin beneath them serve the same purpose for the rest of the legs.

具足 *Gusoku*

ABOVE *Battle in the Bath House*
Battle in the Bath House by Jed Henry draws
inspiration from Capcom's iconic fighting game
series *Street Fighter*, particularly the classic *Street
Fighter II* from 1991. The three-panel format is
distinctly reminiscent of ukiyo-e triptychs
depicting samurai battles and incidents.

BELOW Mitsurugi Heishiro ソウルキャリバー
from the *Soulcalibur* series of fighting games by
Bandai Namco, released between 1995 and 2018.
Mitsurugi, who appears in every game, is a
fictional peasant who takes up the sword and
becomes a mercenary. The character was inspired
by Miyamoto Musashi.

The Duel between Miyamoto Musashi and Tsukahara Bokuden Roo by ukiyo-e master Tsukioka Yoshitoshi depicts a fictional fight between Musashi and Tsukahara Bokuden Roo (Roo means old man), which couldn't have taken place because the latter died before the former was born. According to the myth, Tsukahara deflected Musashi's sword strike with the lid of an iron cooking pot.

月岡 芳年 Tsukiyoka Yoshitoshi (1839–1892)

Captured from PlayStation®4 Pro. 4k images require a 4k display.

Captured from PlayStation®4 Pro. 4k images require a 4k display.

Ghost of Tsushima: The year is 1274. The legendary samurai warriors have to defend Japan when the fearsome Mongol Empire invades the island of Tsushima, wreaking havoc and conquering the local population. As one of the last surviving samurai, the player rises from the ashes to fight back.

Princess Mononoke もののけ姫

Hayao Miyazaki's *Princess Mononoke* (*Mononoke-hime*, 1997) is one of Studio Ghibli's most beloved anime films. The fantasy set in the Muromachi period (1336–1573) tells the tale of an Emishi (indigenous people of northern Japan) village attacked first by a demon and then a daimyo's samurai army.

マシュ

―――はい。
あなたに勝利を、マスター！

Fate/Grand Order
フェイト・グランドオーダー
Images of "servants" (characters) from
the hugely successful *Fate/Grand Order*
mobile role-playing combat game
produced by Sony subsidiary Aniplex.
Many of the characters are drawn from
Japanese history and mythology, and
include incarnations of Miyamoto
Musashi and Minamoto no Raiko
(Minamoto no Yorimitsu). Spin-off
anime, manga, films, video games and
even stage plays have been produced.

Afro Samurai アフロサムライ
Beginning life as an amateur manga by Takashi
Okazaki, the genre-bending, hip-hop-infused *Afro
Samurai* stories of a futuristic black samurai became
an anime series and an Emmy-nominated TV movie
with the title character voiced by Samuel L. Jackson.

CHAPTER 13

THE LEGACY OF THE SAMURAI IN MODERN JAPAN AND BEYOND

The impact of history on a nation is always open to interpretation, as is the history itself. It may be the case that the representations of the samurai which loom large in the psyche of some Japanese, and people around the globe, are to no small extent idealized and romanticized, but their influence has been very real.

As academic and former journalist Andrew Horvat put it in a 2018 paper *Bushido and the Legacy of "Samurai Values" in Contemporary Japan*: "All the same, samurai pop culture heroes are useful: they not only gauge popularly held views of the samurai, but they also provide examples of the virtues which the general public considers to be typical of the noblest traits of the former warrior class."

The end of the *bushi* as the ruling class was heralded by the Meiji Restoration of 1868, led though it was by young samurai. Feudalism was abolished in 1871 and two years later the system of stipends for samurai was ended with a one-off payment in government bonds and a professional army established. In 1876, the Haitorei Edict was issued, forbidding the public carrying of swords by anyone except former daimyo, soldiers and the police.

All this was not the true official end of the samurai, as they were reclassified as shizoku, a new social class that acknowledged their warrior ancestry and that would last until its abolition in 1947 by Supreme Commander for the Allied Powers, General Douglas MacArthur. This was part of wide-reaching American efforts to democratize postwar Japan and rid it of the vestiges of imperialistic, militaristic and feudalistic influence. While the occupying authorities were mostly successful on these fronts, nostalgia for and admiration of the samurai was never quite eradicated.

Initially, in the post-feudal era, their influence on society was far more direct. Former samurai and their descendants abounded in the worlds of politics, education, business and other influential spheres long after their class was dissolved. Having been the most educated and privileged strata of society, this comes as little surprise.

Kumagai no Jiro Naozane (1141–1208), a famed Minamoto retainer, being played by kabuki actor Bando Hikosaburo V in the mid-19th century.

豊原 国周 Toyohara Kunichika (1835–1900)

SAMURAI LOOKING TO THE WEST AND FINDING NEW CAREERS

The new Meiji government had set a course of rapid national modernization, and to that end dispatched a series of study tours, which doubled as diplomatic missions to renegotiate lopsided trade treaties, to the Western nations it was determined to emulate in many respects.

The most significant of these was the Iwakura Mission, which traveled to America and Europe between 1871 and 1873, gathering information on the latest in technology, military matters, medicine, education, law and parliamentary democracy. Led by Iwakura Tomomi, the 50 or so participants included a number of senior statesman who would go on to help shape the new Japan, such as Okubo Toshimichi, Kido Takayoshi, Ito Hirobumi, Kaneko Kentaro and Makino Nobuaki, all of whom were of samurai birth.

The mission was accompanied by around the same number of students, some of whom were young children, who were left overseas to complete their education before bringing the knowledge they acquired back to Japan. In a sign of the relative progressiveness of the time compared with the feudal era, a number of the students were women (some of whom would go on to be pioneers in Japanese female education), but most of them were also of samurai stock.

Former samurai founded some of the most prestigious new private universities of the second half of the 19th century, including Tokyo's Keio University and Waseda University, which between them have produced no fewer than 10 Japanese prime ministers and numerous other senior politicians.

In the 1870s, what would go on to be Japan's three largest newspapers were established and staffed in large numbers by those born into warrior families. While the media might not seem an obvious choice of profession for them, it should be remembered that they were society's most literate strata and a majority of readers would have shared their roots. Horvat suggests in his paper that the relative docility towards power that characterizes the Japanese press to this

day must be understood in the context of its samurai origins, in which loyalty to authority was deeply ingrained.

It should be noted that by no means were all former *bushi* successful. Indeed, so many of the samurai who attempted to use their government pay-off to go into business—a field most had previously viewed with naked disdain—failed so abjectly that they became something of a byword for mercantile haplessness.

The shizoku fared better in politics, an arena where the skill sets they had acquired during the centuries of the Edo period were more applicable. It was often the former samurai who led the push back against what they saw as the excessive Westernization which had accompanied the headlong rush to modernization. An example of this was the 1890 Imperial Rescript on Education (Kyoiku Chokugo), which set out to put traditional values of loyalty, virtue and filial piety, a hark back to the age of the samurai, at the heart of learning.

BUSHIDO RISING

This period also saw rising awareness and discussion of Bushido, mostly by writers and intellectuals who had been born into the samurai class, as something that explained and set the Japanese apart from other nationalities (despite the fact that its notions were in reality at least in part borrowed from an idealized vision of English knights and gentlemen).

After defeating China in a war sparked by friction on the Korean Peninsula in 1894, Japan surprised the world by doing the same to Russia a decade later, thereby becoming the first non-Western international power of the modern age. It was during this time that Bushido became a propaganda tool used to inspire both the civilian population and military personnel. It also shaped the perception of Japan in the West, where the emergence of an Asian nation on the global stage required explanation, something a militaristic code of honor said to define a society helped provide.

The death of the Meiji Emperor in 1912 was accompanied by a display of samurai values that

Ninja Manabe Rokuro, attempting to kill warlord Oda Nobunaga in his castle. Images from ukiyo-e woodblock prints influenced 20th-century pop culture ninja portrayals.

歌川 豊宣 Utagawa Toyonobu (1859–1886)

shocked many and inspired others. Nogi Maresuke, a distinguished general and veteran of the Satsuma Rebellion, the Sino-Japanese War and the Russo-Japanese War, committed *junshi* (following one's master in death by seppuku) alongside his wife as the funeral procession left the Imperial Palace in Tokyo. It is almost needless to say that Nogi was born a samurai.

During the subsequent Taisho era there was a waning of interest in samurai values among the public and intellectuals, though it began to be taught in the public school curriculum and in military education. Historian Oleg Benesch, whose scholarship has done much to provoke a re-examination of the Japanese way of the warrior in the West, referred to 1914 as "the end of the first Bushido boom."

In and after World War I, where Japan fought on

the side of the Allies, there was little heard of Bushido from the nation's friends or foes. In fact, Japan was known for its humane treatment of prisoners of war during the conflicts against China and Russia, as well as in World War I, which some Japanese attributed to Bushido. This was in stark contrast to the reputation of Japanese troops during its imperial expansion and World War II.

Early 1920s Japan had been a place of relative cosmopolitan liberalness, at least among urban elites, and a time where parliamentary democracy flourished. The beginning of the Showa era at the end of 1925 marked a shift toward nationalism, imperialism and militarism, accompanied by a resurgence of Bushido that would help drive Japan to war.

There is perhaps no more obvious symbol of the promulgation of samurai values and Bushido as a tool of imperialism than the issuing of *shin gunto* (new military sword) to military officers between 1935 and 1945. Though these swords were mass-produced mediocre imitations of the katana of old, the message was unequivocal: those wearing them were the new samurai, fighting for the emperor and the sacred nation.

The harsh treatment of captured soldiers, an unwillingness to surrender, kamikaze attacks, suicides by civilians and seppuku by military personnel of the Pacific War have all been explained through the prism of Bushido and samurai heritage. Though the truth is certainly more nuanced, there is little doubt they were factors.

POSTWAR

The crushing defeat suffered in 1945 and subsequent humiliation of occupation led the majority of Japanese to view the militarism and its accompanying tenets of Bushido that had taken the country down that path as a source of pain and shame. Combined with the ban on everything from martial arts to samurai movies, there was a drastic shift away from nostalgia for such values.

But soon after the occupation ended in 1952, samurai were back in force on screen, on the page, on

stage and therefore in the public imagination. Their impact would go on to reverberate in areas of society both predictable and less expected.

From the devastation of World War II, Japan fashioned an economic miracle the likes of which has few parallels. Between 1955 and 1972, Japan's GDP grew by an average of more than 9% annually, taking a war-ravaged industrial basket case to the world's second-largest economy by 1968, a position it would hold until overtaken by China in 2011.

The engine of this rapid rise in wealth and living standards were the workers and salarymen who toiled long hours, eschewed holidays and displayed a loyalty to their companies that has drawn inevitable comparisons with the samurai. Professor Yoshioka Hiroshi argued in a 1995 essay *Samurai and Self-colonization in Japan* that many Japanese reveled in the image of themselves as modern samurai and even enjoyed being caricatured in such fashion in the West. "The world of business is often described as a battlefield, in which a strong and loyal male subject of production is celebrated as a samurai. Every month many business magazines feature success stories of business champions, comparing them to a shogun in the Sengoku period, or even stories of a shogun comparing him to an executive at Sony or Toyota," wrote Yoshioka.

When Japanese workers literally work themselves to death, referred to as *karoshi*, or commit suicide due to employment-related stresses, it adds fuel to the fire of the perception of a *bushi*-like devotion to their company or organization (a stand-in for daimyo). The relatively high rates of suicide in Japan, which have fallen sharply in recent years, have also been explained in terms of the samurai tradition.

Admiration for samurai and claims of adherence to Bushido has also made its presence felt in the underground economy. Among yakuza gangsters, whose membership peaked at more than 180,000 in the 1960s, there are those who see themselves to be guardians of the samurai tradition. Some clans refer to themselves as *ninkyo dantai* (chivalrous organizations) and believe they live according to the samurai ideals of *giri-ninjo*. *Giri* contains meanings of honor, social obligation and duty, though it is difficult to translate concisely into other languages, while *ninjo* is human feelings; it is following the former at the expense of the latter that characterized the samurai loyalty which some yakuza aspire to. Contemporary gang bosses have been known to lament the decline of *giri-ninjo* among the younger generation.

Perhaps more predictably, members of ultra-nationalist groups (*uyoku-dantai*), which are closely intertwined with the yakuza, also wax lyrical about Bushido and samurai values in their nostalgia for the perceived glory of Japan's past.

An extreme example of such nostalgia was the celebrated author Yukio Mishima, who spoke eloquently and often of the decline of warrior ideals in Westernized modern Japan. With the aim of overturning the constitution, which was effectively imposed by the US in 1947, and restoring the emperor, Mishima formed a small militia and on November 25, 1970, attempted a coup d'état at a Self-Defense Forces barracks in Tokyo.

After taking the commander hostage and making a speech to the assembled troops from a balcony, Mishima was roundly jeered, as he appeared to have expected would happen. He then set about committing seppuku, only for the young man acting as his second, and reportedly his lover, to repeatedly botch the beheading. Another militiaman stepped in and beheaded Mishima and then the original *kaishaku*, who had also cut his own stomach open.

THE BUSHI IN THE 21ST CENTURY

The legacy of the samurai continues to make its presence felt in Japan and in the ways the nation and its citizenry are perceived abroad. Impressions of an inscrutable, Oriental otherness can still be found in

reporting by the Western media. Though of course not all of that is due to Japan's samurai past, it remains a convenient trope.

The emergency crews which tackled the triple meltdowns at the Fukushima Dai-ichi nuclear plant after the giant tsunami of March 2011 were dubbed the "Fukushima 50" outside Japan and one Australian newspaper referred to them as "nameless samurai" in its headline.

And it is not only in the West where such notions exist. In 2009, conferences on Bushido in China and Taiwan attracted more than 100 academics from around Asia. Whether for reasons of political expedience or genuine fear, Chinese academia in particular has produced considerable quantities of work on the subject, often portraying Bushido as an explanation for a perceived inherent militarism in Japan. Such supposed tendencies are less than evident in the problems experienced by the Japan Self-Defense Force, which has failed to hit its recruiting targets every year for the last decade. The shortfall has been between 25 and 30% in recent years and it has taken to using anime characters in its recruitment advertising, but no samurai imagery.

Now sufficiently divorced and rehabilitated from associations with wartime propaganda, samurai characters remained deeply embedded in Japanese culture and are used to promote a wide range of products. Displays of *kabuto* helmets, *yoroi* armor and katana are still common for the May 5th Children's Day (formerly Boy's Day) celebrations to symbolize strength and courage.

Illustrative of the modern affection for all things samurai was the result of a public poll taken in late 2005 to choose a nickname for the Japan national soccer team. Beating out its nearest rival by two to one was Samurai Blue.

PHOTO CREDITS

Pages 111 & 112 © The Trustees of the British Museum c/o Scala, Florence
Page 113 © Museum of Fine Arts, Boston - Bequest of Maxim Karolik - 64.817
Pages 114–115 © Museum of Fine Arts, Boston - William Sturgis Bigelow Collection - 11.41356a-c
Page 117 © Los Angeles County Museum of Art - Herbert R. Cole Collection - M.84.31.244 / Digital Image Museum Associates / LACMA / Art Resource NY / Scala, Florence
Pages 118–119 © Library of Congress, Prints & Photographs Division [repr. number: LC-DIG-jpd-01638] (loc.gov/item/2008660444/)
Page 121 © Photo courtesy National Gallery of Victoria, Melbourne
Pages 122–123 © CPA Media Pte Ltd / Alamy Stock Photo
Page 125 © The Trustees of the British Museum c/o Scala, Florence
Page 126 © Library of Congress, Prints & Photographs Division [repr. number: LC-DIG-jpd-00429] (loc.gov/item/2009615416/)
Page 127 © Artokoloro / Alamy Stock Photo
Page 129 © Library of Congress, Prints & Photographs Division [repr. number: LC-DIG-jpd-01786] (loc.gov/item/2002700059/)
Page 130 © The Trustees of the British Museum c/o Scala, Florence
Page 131 © The Trustees of the British Museum c/o Scala, Florence
Page 132 © Matteo Omied / Alamy Stock Photo
Page 133 © CPA Media Pte Ltd / Alamy Stock Photo
Pages 134–135 © The Metropolitan Museum of Art / Art Resource / Scala, Florence - JP3558
Page 136 © Public Domain
Page 137 © Historical Views / agefotostock / Alamy Stock Photo
Page 139 © Universal Art Archive / Alamy Stock Photo
Page 140 © Tsukioka Yoshitoshi, Obata Sukerokuro Nobuyo Commits Harakiri, 1868 - Ink on Paper - 14 5/16 in. x 9 11/16 in. (363.54 mm x 246.06 mm) - Scripps College, Claremont, California, USA - Gift of Mr. Fred Marer
Page 141 © The Trustees of the British Museum c/o Scala, Florence
Pages 142–143 © CPA Media Pte Ltd / Alamy Stock Photo
Pages 144, 145, 146, 147 & 148–149 © CPA Media Pte Ltd / Alamy Stock Photo
Page 151 © The Metropolitan Museum of Art / Art Resource / Scala, Florence - 2019.420.12
Page 153 © The Trustees of the British Museum c/o Scala, Florence
Page 154–155 © Photo courtesy National Gallery of Victoria, Melbourne
Pages 156–157 © CPA Media Pte Ltd / Alamy Stock Photo
Pages 158 & 159 © Universal Images Group via Getty Images
Pages 160 © Sepia Times / Universal Images Group via Getty Images
Page 161 © Felice Beato / Hulton Archive / Getty Images
Page 162 © Wilhelm Burger / Imagno / Getty Images
Page 163 © Hulton Archive / Stringer / Getty Images
Pages 166–167 © Heritage Image Partnership Ltd / Alamy Stock Photo
Pages 168–169 © The Metropolitan Museum of Art / Art Resource / Scala, Florence - JP3567
Page 170 top © Artokoloro / Alamy Stock Photo
Page 170 bottom © Public Domain
Page 171 © Museum of Fine Arts, Boston - Gift of Louis Aaron Lebowich - 50.2922a-b
Page 172 top © Artokoloro / Alamy Stock Photo
Page 172 bottom © Pump Park Vintage Photography / Alamy Stock Photo
Page 173 © Michael Maslan / Corbis / VCG via Getty Images
Pages 174 & 175 top © MeijiShowa / Alamy Stock Photo
Page 175 bottom © Getty Images
Page 177 © Allstar Picture Library Ltd. / Alamy Stock Photo
Page 180 © Ashmolean Museum / Heritage Images / Getty Images
Page 181 © Toho Company / Photo 12 / Alamy Stock Photo
Page 182 © TCD/Prod.DB / Alamy Stock Photo
Page 183 © AF Archive / Alamy Stock Photo
Page 184 © Toho Company / Photo 12 / Alamy Stock Photo
Page 185 top © Pictorial Press Ltd / Alamy Stock Photo
Page 185 bottom © Allstar Picture Library Ltd. / Alamy Stock Photo
Pages 186 & 187 © LMPC via Getty Images
Page 188 top © Allstar Picture Library Ltd. / Alamy Stock Photo
Pages 188 bottom; 189 © Movie Poster Image Art / Getty Images
Page 190 © Shochiku Eiga / Photo 12 / Alamy Stock Photo
Page 191 top © AF Archive / Alamy Stock Photo
Page 191 bottom © TNM Image Archives / Tokyo National Museum (webarchives. tnm.jp/imgsearch/show/C0095286)
Page 192 © Columbia Pictures / Getty Images
Page 193 © TCD/Prod.DB / Alamy Stock Photo
Page 194 © Museum of Fine Arts, Boston - William Sturgis Bigelow Collection - 11.30343

Page 195 © United Archives GmbH / Alamy Stock Photo
Page 196 © Greenwich Film Productions / Photo 12 / Alamy Stock Photo
Page 197 top © Collection Christophel / Alamy Stock Photo
Page 197 bottom © United Archives GmbH / Alamy Stock Photo
Page 198 top © Allstar Picture Library Ltd. / Alamy Stock Photo
Page 198 bottom © CPA Media Pte Ltd / Alamy Stock Photo
Page 199 © AF Archive / Alamy Stock Photo
Pages 200–201 © Moviestore Collection Ltd / Alamy Stock Photo
Page 202 © The Trustees of the British Museum c/o Scala, Florence
Page 203 top © AF Archive / Alamy Stock Photo
Page 204 © Photo 12 / Alamy Stock Photo
Page 203 bottom; 204 © Photo 12 / Alamy Stock Photo
Page 205 © Entertainment Pictures / Alamy Stock Photo
Pages 206–207 top © Collection Christophel / Alamy Stock Photo
Pages 206–207 bottom © PictureLux / The Hollywood Archive / Alamy Stock Photo
Pages 210–211 © Ghost of Tsushima™ 2020-2021 Sony Interactive Entertainment LLC. Published by Sony Interactive Entertainment Europe Limited. Developed by Sucker Punch Productions, LLC. "Ghost of Tsushima" is a trademark of Sony Interactive Entertainment LLC. All rights reserved.
Page 212 © Collezione privata
Page 213 © LONE WOLF AND CUB (©) KAZUO KOIKE / GOSEKI KOJIMA (©) / Per l'edizione italiana © Panini SpA
Pages 214; 215; 216; 217 © Fair use
Page 218 left top © The British Museum, London, Distr. RMN-Grand Palais / The Trustees of the British Museum - 2008,3037.15401
Page 218 left bottom © Public domain, The Metropolitan Museum of Art
Page 218 right top & bottom © Fair use (bramblescrossing)
Page 219 © Capcom-Digital Bros
Page 220 © ArcadeImages / Alamy Stock Photo
Page 221 © Kochmedia
Page 222 left © The British Museum, London, Distr. RMN-Grand Palais / The Trustees of the British Museum - 2008,3037.15009
Pages 222 right; 223 right; 224 top © Jed Henry / UkiyoeHeroes.com
Page 223 left © Public domain, The Metropolitan Museum of Art
Page 224 bottom © SOULCALIBUR™&©BANDAI NAMCO Entertainment Inc.
Page 225 © Photo courtesy National Gallery of Victoria, Melbourne
Page 226–227 © Ghost of Tsushima™ ©2020-2021 Sony Interactive Entertainment LLC. Published by Sony Interactive Entertainment Europe Limited. Developed by Sucker Punch Productions, LLC. "Ghost of Tsushima" is a trademark of Sony Interactive Entertainment LLC. All rights reserved.
Page 228 © AF Archive / Alamy Stock Photo
Page 229 top © Studio Ghibli / Photo 12 / Alamy Stock Photo
Page 229 bottom © United Archives GmbH / Alamy Stock Photo
Page 230 top © Kiyoshi Ota / Bloomberg via Getty Images
Page 230 bottom © Heorshe / Alamy Stock Photo
Page 231 © Moviestore Collection Ltd / Alamy Stock Photo
Page 235 © CPA Media Pte Ltd / Alamy Stock Photo
Page 237 © Museum of Fine Arts, Boston - William Sturgis Bigelow Collection - 11.34914

ACKNOWLEDGMENTS

Jed Henry, UkiyoeHeroes.com - Elisa Panzani, Panini SpA - Lorenzo Baccile, Michaela Foster e Alfredo Mazziotta, Sony Interactive Entertainment Italy - Kirstie Morey, Art Gallery of South Australia - Clémence Oliviero, Alexandra De Bonis e Masakazu Yoshiba, Bandai Namco Entertainment Europe - Lisa L. Crane, The Claremont Colleges Library - Margalit Monroe e John Trendler, Ruth Chandler Williamson Gallery / Scripps College - Yasumichi Kuniya, DNP Art Communications Co., Ltd., Tokyo - Jennifer E. Berry, Freer Gallery of Art and Arthur M. Sackler Gallery - Fabrizio Faraoni, Halifax/Digital Bros - Britt Bowen, Monique Goodin e Jeff Steward, Harvard Art Museums - Sara Sacchi, Kochmedia - Carolyn Cruthirds, Museum of Fine Arts, Boston - Sigourney Jacks e Philip White, National Gallery of Victoria - Jonathan Hoppe, Philadelphia Museum of Art - Sébastien Felmann, Leïla Audouy, Tiphaine Leroux e Christophe Mauberret, Agence photographique de la Réunion des Musées Nationaux (RMN)-Grand Palais, Paris - Laura Giuntini, SCALA Picture Library - Kaoru Morimura, Tuttle-Mori Agency, Inc.

Published by Tuttle Publishing, an imprint of Periplus Editions (HK) Ltd

www.tuttlepublishing.com

Original edition:
Samurai - Dall'*ukiyoe* alla cultura pop © Nuinui SA 2021
Editorial Director Federica Romagnoli
Graphic Design and Production Clara Zanotti

ISBN 978-4-8053-1659-7

Library of Congress Cataloging in Process

English Translation © 2022 Periplus Editions (HK) Ltd

Distributed by

North America, Latin America & Europe
Tuttle Publishing
364 Innovation Drive
North Clarendon, VT 05759-9436 U.S.A.
Tel: 1 (802) 773-8930
Fax: 1 (802) 773-6993
info@tuttlepublishing.com
www.tuttlepublishing.com

Japan
Tuttle Publishing
Yaekari Building 3rd Floor, 5-4-12 Osaki
Shinagawa-ku, Tokyo 141-0032
Tel: (81) 3 5437-0171; Fax: (81) 3 5437-0755
sales@tuttle.co.jp; www.tuttle.co.jp

Asia Pacific
Berkeley Books Pte. Ltd.
3 Kallang Sector, #04-01, Singapore 349278
Tel: (65) 67412178; Fax: (65) 67412179
inquiries@periplus.com.sg; www.tuttlepublishing.com

Printed in China   2304EP
25 24 23   10 9 8 7 6 5 4 3 2

"Books to Span the East and West"

Tuttle Publishing was founded in 1832 in the small New England town of Rutland, Vermont [USA]. Our core values remain as strong today as they were then—to publish best-in-class books which bring people together one page at a time. In 1948, we established a publishing outpost in Japan—and Tuttle is now a leader in publishing English-language books about the arts, languages and cultures of Asia. The world has become a much smaller place today and Asia's economic and cultural influence has grown. Yet the need for meaningful dialogue and information about this diverse region has never been greater. Over the past seven decades, Tuttle has published thousands of books on subjects ranging from martial arts and paper crafts to language learning and literature—and our talented authors, illustrators, designers and photographers have won many prestigious awards. We welcome you to explore the wealth of information available on Asia at **www.tuttlepublishing.com**.

RIGHT The woodcut of the master Utagawa Kuniyoshi depicts Matsui Tamijiro fighting against a gigantic snake, a topic represented in various ukiyo-e prints.

歌川 国芳 Utagawa Kuniyoshi (1798–1861)

BACK ENDPAPERS *UFO Robot Grendizer*
ＵＦＯロボ グレンダイザー
The *UFO Robot Grendizer* manga followed the familiar path to anime series, anime films and associated merchandise in the mid-1970s. The series was a hit in France, where it was titled *Goldorak*, and Italy, where it was known as *Goldrake*. The aesthetics of the robots and their combat drew heavily on samurai influences. In the US, toys based on robots from the series were sold as part of the Shogun Warriors line.

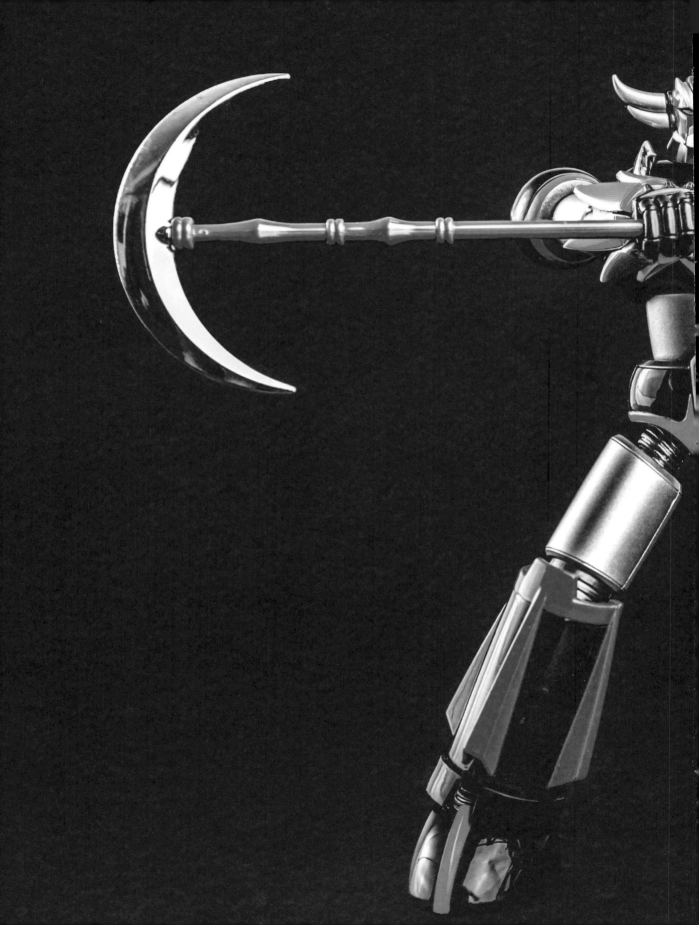